IMMERSION

Chicago Guides
to *Writing*, Editing,
and Publishing

IMMERSION

A Writer's Guide to Going Deep

vvv
vv
v

TED CONOVER

THE UNIVERSITY OF CHICAGO PRESS

Chicago and London

The University of Chicago Press, Chicago 60637

The University of Chicago Press, Ltd., London

© 2016 by Ted Conover

All rights reserved. Published 2016.

Printed in the United States of America

25 24 23 22 21 20 19 18 17 16   1 2 3 4 5

ISBN-13: 978-0-226-41616-8 (cloth)

ISBN-13: 978-0-226-11306-7 (paper)

ISBN-13: 978-0-226-11323-4 (e-book)

DOI: 10.7208/chicago/9780226113234.001.0001

Library of Congress Cataloging-in-Publication Data

Names: Conover, Ted, author.

Title: Immersion : a writer's guide to going deep / Ted Conover.

Other titles: Chicago guides to writing, editing, and publishing.

Description: Chicago ; London : The University of Chicago Press, 2016. | Series:

Chicago guides to writing, editing, and publishing | Includes bibliographical

references and index.

Identifiers: LCCN 2016015885| ISBN 9780226416168 (cloth : alk. paper) |

ISBN 9780226113067 (pbk. : alk. paper) | ISBN 9780226113234 (e-book)

Subjects: LCSH: Reportage literature–Authorship. | Participant observation. |

Investigative reporting. | Creative nonfiction.

Classification: LCC PN3377.5.R45 C66 2016 | DDC 808.02–dc23

LC record available at https://lccn.loc.gov/2016015885

♾ This paper meets the requirements of ANSI/NISO Z39.48-1992

(Permanence of Paper).

For Asa and Nell

CONTENTS

Go talk with those who are rumored to be unlike you,

And whom, it is said, you are so unlike . . .

. . . Let the new sound in our streets be the patient sound

Of your discourse.

RICHARD P. WILBUR

(from the poem "For the Student Strikers,"
written for the *Wesleyan Strike News*,
Spring 1970)

INTRODUCTION

Turn and face the strange.

DAVID BOWIE

For me it started on a train.

I hopped it in the old Missouri Pacific yard in St. Louis. I was 22 years old and had little idea what I was doing. In the movies, hoboes always boarded trains that were moving, and so that was my plan: sit in the weeds, out of sight, and wait for a train going slow enough that I might grab ahold and climb aboard.

It took me more than a day to catch a train. The victory of my first freight-hop—into an open-topped gondola car—became a defeat about ten minutes later, when the string of cars was parked at a siding just outside the yard.

But then another came by, and finally I hopped a real freight (westbound, as luck would have it—by that point, I would have departed in any direction). To me the ride was like a prelude, a passage into another country. When, two days after that, I finally met up with a hobo and began to travel with him, I felt my journey had truly begun.

vvv

I had no idea, at the time, that I would one day write a book about my experience—nobody I had met in my life, to my knowledge, outside of professors, had written a book. But I did have a plan to write about it, first in the form of diary-like "field notes," and then, if my professors thought I had enough material, in the form of an undergraduate anthropology thesis.

1

Getting that far had been a struggle. My advisor pointed out, quite reasonably, that riding freight trains was dangerous and against the law. Bad things could happen to me. I said I understood that. Therefore, he wouldn't be comfortable supervising my research. I remember his wooden office chair creaking in the silence that followed. I couldn't argue him into feeling comfortable. And yet I could tell he wasn't quite finished. We both sat for a while longer. "On the other hand, if you were to withdraw from the college for a semester, do this on your own, and take notes, we could consider it upon your return." I had never been so happy with a "maybe" in my life.

Months later, back from the journey, I presented my notes, we discussed a structure, and they said yes. They suggested I avoid the first person voice, but agreed to my including a chapter at the end about what the research had been like for me. My model for this was a book I had read in the meantime, *Tally's Corner: A Study of Negro Streetcorner Men*, by Elliot Liebow; I titled my final chapter just as he had his appendix: "A Field Experience in Retrospect."

Few of my friends were as interested in my thesis, which considered matters such as hobo perceptions of time and space, as they were by stories of my experience. "Were you ever scared?" "Did you get arrested?" "Who were the main people you traveled with?" I wrote an article for a student magazine about one morning with a hobo in California's Sierra Nevada mountains. The college alumni magazine reprinted it, and the national media started calling. To make a long story short, I was able to get a book contract—essentially to rewrite my thesis in narrative form, as a chronological first-person story with characters and incidents. That became *Rolling Nowhere*.

Both during my research for the thesis and during the writing of the book I had many questions. My small college had no courses on ethnography and did not encourage students to do field work:

How would I take notes? What would I take notes about? My advisor gave me a book he had just received from its publisher, called *Participant Observation*. It explained about field methods, what to look for and think about, and I carried it on my rail travels. As for writing my own book: I had written some newspaper features and short magazine articles. But a book—where would I begin? There were many authors I admired, and I read some of their books along the way and after—*In Patagonia*, by Bruce Chatwin; *Blue Highways*, by William Least Heat-Moon; *Bound for Glory*, by Woody Guthrie; *Down and Out in Paris and London*, by George Orwell. I got something different from fiction, from *On the Road*, by Jack Kerouac, and *The Road*, by Jack London, to Anne Tyler's *The Accidental Tourist* and fiction by Bobbie Ann Mason that I read in *Harper's*. Doing this, I kind of began a private conversation with each book and short story about what I might take from it ("I admired *this*, but not so much *that*"). I was looking for a model, for ways to write, ways to *speak*. Nothing seemed directly applicable to my project but looking back, all of it helped some. In the end, like any other writer, I had to go it alone.

Over the years, I've returned to immersive projects like riding the rails again and again. One reason is that I like to learn via experience: to imagine a situation that will teach me something. I find exploring social worlds to be deeply rewarding. With different parents, in a different place or time, my life would have been so different; could I have managed, I've often wondered, to live in *that* way, or *that*? What is life like for *those* people? The more I wrote, the more I learned about how to research and how to write. I began to teach. As younger writers continued to ask me for guidance, I decided to try to commit to paper some of the advice I share with them.

ᴠᴠᴠ

This book is the result. The best way to summarize it, I suppose, is that it's the book I wish I had in hand when I set off to ride the rails. Generally speaking, it's about what I call immersion writing: work that grows out of a writer's efforts to learn about somebody else's world by placing himself in it for a while. For my purposes, most such work is narrative: reflection is allowed, even *required*, but the main project is to write stories, not essays.

I've written this book for younger versions of me. I've written it for anybody who might want to give such a project a try. Previous accomplishment is not a requirement (though some courses in journalism, writing, or creative writing might help). I imagine most of my readers to be in college, or beyond (but even that is not a real requirement). Some will be students who are not focused on getting published. Others will be college graduates, or those with advanced degrees, who are. I write for my peers, and think of my peers as aspiring writers of approximately 18–90 years of age who want to write something of value that others might want to read. If that thing of value is a class assignment, fine. If it's a long article for a newspaper or magazine, also fine. If it's a book for an audience of general readers, extra good.

Let me also say that when I talk about writers, I'm thinking about documentarians working in other media as well, such as podcasts, video, and film. Those fields too allow for immersive research and narrative storytelling, and I hope their practitioners might ignore the exclusive reference to "writing" in the pages that follow.

vvv

The six chapters that follow will walk you through all the steps of an immersive project.

Chapter 1, Why Immerse?, will consider the particular character and opportunities of immersion, and define the enterprise in a little more detail. The kind of writing I'm talking about has a literary history—we'll talk about important ancestors—and it has literary cousins: ethnography, travel writing, memoir. We'll take a look at each of them.

In chapter II, Choosing a Subject and Gaining Access, we'll jump right in, looking at what subjects work best for this sort of writing. Then we will consider what's next: You've dropped off your freight train in a new town and you notice somebody else doing the same. He's walking your way: *now* what do you do?

Chapter III, Once Inside, has two parts. The first, Us & Them, looks at broad questions of how to immerse, from self-presentation to ethics in relationships. The second part, What to Look For, picks up more specific, practical questions around this kind of research. What will you ask about? How will you hope to spend time? Is your job to be a fly on the wall or something more active? How will you know which details are important and which are not? And how will you take notes? Beyond just understanding a new social world, it helps to anticipate how you might render it in prose once you're finished. In other words, research is not just about coming to understand, it's about pausing now and then to take the measure of your research and imagine how it will translate onto the page. My shorthand for this idea is "reporting for story."

Chapter IV considers an important subset of immersive writing: undercover research. Not telling your subjects who you really are or what you're really there for raises a host of ethical questions. What subjects justify this controversial practice? Undercover reporting has unique power and advantages that we'll consider alongside its profound drawbacks.

Chapter V, Writing It, has two parts as well. The first, The Narrator, considers who is speaking, a first person voice or a third person, and either way, how do we realize an effective narrative persona? The second part, Structure, considers the troublesome question of putting it all together. A series of concrete examples looks at ways to render the passage of time, the importance of characters and how to depict them, the value of scenes, the appeal of trouble, and thoughts about beginnings and endings.

Finally, chapter VI, Aftermath, is a brief consideration of finishing. If publication is your goal and you succeed, congratulations! But success can have complications—such as what happens when your subjects read about themselves. I talk about how to prep subjects for this moment, so that they aren't surprised, and about fact-checking. And finally I talk about de-immersing: seeing how it feels to be back in our old clothes—just right? Or is it time to buy some new ones?

vvv

As you can see, this book is not a how-to for the nitty-gritty of pitching, revising, getting an agent, or publicizing. It's about something at once more specialized and more meaningful: creating a great piece of immersion writing. When you've got the goods, by which I mean something original, unusual, and beautifully executed, I believe the rest will follow.

Immersion writing has huge potential for sowing empathy in the world. It's a way to introduce readers to strangers and to make them care, a way to shine a light into places that need it. But how to do the research, and how to turn that research into prose, are by no means obvious; there are many ways to go astray. This is not a field manual, exactly, nor is it a map; no one guide could cover all the wilderness, all the unknowns lying in wait for an adventurous writer. You'll make your own path. I'll be pleased if this might serve as a headlamp.

I. WHY IMMERSE?

> If you just learn a single trick, Scout, you'll get along
> a lot better with all kinds of folks. You never really understand
> a person until you consider things from his point of view ...
> until you climb inside of his skin and walk around in it.
>
> HARPER LEE, *To Kill a Mockingbird*

How to think about strangers is one of the conundrums of human existence. The warning parents give children, *don't speak to strangers*, may be good advice when it comes to unknown adults. But how about other kids? What is school, for most of us, other than a first experience of immersion among contemporaries we don't know? And when does it become okay to speak to strangers — ever?

Many of us are nervous around others. We are slow to "put ourselves out there," wary of entanglements or rejection. We hang out with our own kind.

Shyness is natural, but not necessarily a good thing. If we can't get past it, our worlds can stay small. My third-grade teacher, whom I loved, tried to get us to think about shyness. She quoted Will Rogers, the American humorist and homespun philosopher: "I never met a man I didn't like."

Wow, really? I thought. Even bad people, bank robbers, murderers? I've been thinking about that idea for almost fifty years.

vvv

I live in New York City, one of America's most stratified metropolises, with vast extremes of wealth and many distinct ethnic identities. I mix with my fellow New Yorkers every day, on the street and on the subway, but the subset of those with whom I have real conversations, actual social discourse, is much, much smaller. Sometimes I think back on the place I'm from, Colorado, and wax nostalgic about how, though the place was less diverse, mixing was somehow easier: something in the air said it was okay, and even expected, to chat with strangers. To be newly arrived was normal. Ethnic enclaves were fewer and seemed to have more permeable membranes. I still remember the day when, home from college in New England, I rented a car at the Denver airport and the guy behind the counter, after we had chatted a few moments, said in apparent mock self-disparagement, "Oh, you probably just think I'm some guido from Brooklyn." I looked at him confused. "What's a guido?" I asked. I'd never heard that phrase for Italian American.

But New York is not all snobbery and specialization. New York, deep in its DNA, has Walt Whitman. Whitman, a poet and journalist, wrote a long and famous poem called "Song of Myself," and another that is wonderful called "Song of the Open Road." Both feature long lists of people he hopes to meet and know. In "Song of Myself" he mentions the duck-shooter, the deacons, the lunatic, the squaw, the deck-hands, the one-year wife, the paving man, the "pedler," the opium-eater, and many more. In "Song of the Open Road" he writes,

> The early market-man, the hearse, the moving of furniture
>   into the town, the return back from the town,
> They pass, I also pass, any thing passes, none can be
>   interdicted.
> None but are accepted, none but shall be dear to me.

When I walk downtown on Broadway, to which Whitman addressed a poem ("What hurrying human tides, or day or night!/ What passions, winnings, losses, ardors, swim thy waters!"), I try to channel him, because in some ways Whitman helps me to understand myself. I like to travel and I like to hang out and Whitman helps me understand why. Whitman, as many Americans still do, nurtured an idea of a country where nobody is better than anybody else, where everyone can meet and engage. It strikes me as a democratic ideal worth keeping alive. When I'm out there talking to people I feel as though I'm emulating, and in turn maybe modeling, a kind of democratic discourse.

Americans don't have a corner on this kind of thinking. An expression in Spanish conveys a related idea: *Cada cabeza es un mundo.* Every mind is a world, a universe. In other words, each of us is interesting. What could be a better calling, in this world, than getting to know other minds?

After my first two books, when I was still living out West, I came to New York and attended a party where David Remnick, who went on to become editor of the *New Yorker*, introduced me as "a writer who makes his living sleeping on the ground." The subjects I had chosen for those first books were groups of people, hoboes and migrant workers, whom you didn't need a lot of money to hang out with. Often in my life, when I've been sleeping on the ground, it means I've been having an adventure, so I think of it as a good thing. The prospect of adventure—of getting out of my circle, my world, my own head for a while—has been another enduring appeal to me of this work. Occasionally somebody who doesn't quite get this will look at me as some kind of a nut, consigned to a lifetime of hardship in the pursuit of my craft. How do you keep doing this? My answer is usually something to the effect of no, you've got it wrong. It's not about the suffering, it's about the opportunity, the chance to learn new things. What could be better than riding freights with hoboes/traveling with migrants/driving a cab in Aspen/working as a meat inspector for a while? And I mean it.

Granted: the difficulty is a given. People don't always want to talk, to let you in. Not everybody you get to know will turn out to be a person you are glad to know. (Sorry, Will Rogers.) Sometimes conditions are uncomfortable. Often there are long stretches of waiting and tedium. You might become lonely, you might get sick. Staying home or going to the office in nice clothes would no doubt be easier. But oh, so much less interesting!

A case in point: one evening when I was working as a guard at Sing Sing prison, I came home, collapsed on the couch, and turned on the TV. I'd had a long day dealing with stubborn and angry prisoners, not to mention fellow correction officers (COs) who had second-guessed some of my decisions in a way I would not describe as supportive. On the screen was a presidential news conference—the reporters looked well-dressed, alert, more engaged than stressed. I'd been in that briefing room years before as an intern at US News & World Report and might have followed that path. The shouting of questions in between the President's answers was a bit chaotic, but nobody in that briefing room was going to get slugged or shanked. Everyone seemed more or less collegial, and briefly I felt envious.

But after a good meal and a hot shower, that feeling went away. What I was doing was unpredictable, trying, sometimes frightening—but almost every single day, I came home having seen or heard something remarkable that my friends could scarcely imagine. One day it was the young inmate who said to me, as I escorted him down the corridor to a medical appointment and asked about his "bid," "CO, I'm gonna be here till the sun burns out." Another day it was the quick response of a fellow officer who saw an inmate run into me and wasn't sure if it had been intentional: if it had, he was ready to subdue him for me, to put his own body on the line, no questions asked. Or the realization that grew over several months about how, despite the fact that I was a small cog in a big correctional machine, I had an important choice to make. As I wrote in Newjack: Guarding Sing Sing, "It took time (and confrontations) to decide (or to discover) what kind of person was going to be wearing your uniform. A hard-ass or a softie? Inmates' friend or inmates' enemy? Straight or crooked? A user of force or a writer of tickets? A strict overseer or a lender of hands? The job was full of discretionary power and the decisions about how to use it were often moral."

Could I have learned that any other way? Well, maybe. But it would have meant less to me as a writer because I would have been hearing about somebody else's experience, not parsing my own.

Research doesn't have to be as secretive or intensely immersive as mine was in prison to yield valuable insights. For chapters on West Bank checkpoints and Nigerian traffic, respectively, in The Routes of Man, I accompanied a student in Ramallah on a weekend visit home to his parents' house in Hebron, and spent several days with an ambulance crew posted to a highway intersection in Lagos. Everybody knew I was a foreign journalist; in those settings (and most others) I could never pretend otherwise. The point is that by simply spending time with people, being at their sides as they encounter challenging situations — by hanging out, in other words — you learn a lot more about them than you might by only conducting interviews. By eating with them, traveling with them, breathing their air, you get more than just information. You gain shared experience. And often you get powerful true stories.

vvv

In the past 50 years, nonfiction writing has undergone a great flowering, as writers borrowed from the storytelling techniques of fiction and otherwise experimented with creative approaches. A watershed moment in terms of immersion writing was 1966–67, which saw the publication of Truman Capote's "nonfiction novel,"

In Cold Blood; Hunter S. Thompson's transgressive and ground-breaking *Hell's Angels: The Strange and Terrible Saga of the Outlaw Motor-cycle Gangs*; and *Paper Lion: Confessions of a Last-String Quarterback*, the most famous of George Plimpton's participatory forays into the world of professional sports.

In *Cold Blood*, though not strictly speaking immersion writing by my definition—Capote did not live with his main subjects, Richard Hickok and Perry Smith, whom he met only after they had been apprehended and charged with murdering an entire family in Holcomb, Kansas—approaches some of the ideals of the form with its intensely empathetic approach. Without ever minimizing the horror of the crimes they committed, Capote nevertheless listened intently to their stories, particularly the life story of Smith, with whom he corresponded for months and developed a deep connection. They may have done something monstrous but they were complicated individuals, not one-dimensional villains. In one stroke, Capote established a new genre, true crime, with an exemplar that still stands as a masterpiece of storytelling. Some of the license he took in reconstructing scenes and dialogue raises eyebrows among nonfiction writers today, but that's a quibble; looking back, this is a book that shook journalism awake, and opened a world of possibilities to writers of my generation. (It should also be said that waiting for the killers' execution, which Capote saw as his book's conclusion and finally witnessed, exacted a huge toll on him.)

Some of the same can be said of Hunter S. Thompson's *Hell's Angels: The Strange and Terrible Saga of the Outlaw Motorcycle Gangs*, though it is a very different kind of book. *Hell's Angels* has a first-person narrator, Thompson, who openly identifies with some of the outsider ethos of his subjects, dabbling with some of the same illegality (e.g., drug use) and not aspiring at all to the sort of sober respectability common among journalists of the time. His willing participation in activities of the Angels for the better part of a year reveals a narrator who is transgressive, smart but countercultural, and clearly placed at risk by his subjects (with whom he parts ways after receiving a beating from a group of them).

Thompson's book began as an assignment for *Rolling Stone* magazine, an important incubator for immersion writing over the years. So did Timothy Crouse's *Boys on the Bus* (1973), an account of life among correspondents covering the 1972 US presidential campaign. Some of Thompson's irreverence and bravado are echoed in Crouse's book, which helped to establish an interest in readers for "behind-the-scenes" accounts by insiders — as had Gay Talese's *The Kingdom and the Power: Behind the Scenes at The New York Times: The Institution That Influences the World* (1969).

The third of these books, George Plimpton's *Paper Lion*, was very different from the other two but also a landmark. The idea was simple but appealing: Plimpton, a somewhat British-sounding blue blood with literary credentials that including cofounding the *Paris Review*, joined the Detroit Lions football team as a participant in preseason training. Using his own incompetence to comic effect, Plimpton paid close attention to certain stand-out personalities, players' off-the-field hijinks, and what it felt like to be part of the group. Though not the first of his participatory forays into professional sports (his 1961 book, *Out of My League*, described a session on the mound pitching to All Stars of the American and National Leagues), it quickly became the best known. Today *Paper Lion* is practically synonymous with "immersion writing" to many readers of a certain age. (The sportswriter Frank Deford and I once shared a literary agent; when the agent introduced us at a social occasion by describing my first two books, Deford exclaimed, "What are you, some kind of proletarian George Plimpton?")

Another milestone work that pushed against the bounds of convention was Tom Wolfe's *The Electric Kool-Aid Acid Test* (1968).

The East Coast journalist traveled West to encounter 1960s luminary Ken Kesey, with whom he roamed the country in a crazily painted bus filled with followers known as the Merry Pranksters. Alongside the Pranksters' drug experiments, Wolfe was conducting a literary one, seeing what it was like to be *of* the group while simultaneously apart. "Despite the skepticism I brought here, I am suddenly experiencing *their* feeling," he writes early on. This "saturation reporting," as Wolfe would later call it, was one of the beginnings of the New Journalism—a style of research where the journalist didn't simply observe with professional detachment, he traveled alongside his subjects, engaging with them over an extended period.

Wolfe's impulse to bring readers into worlds behind image and headline was evident again in *The Right Stuff*, his 1979 book about the astronauts of Project Mercury, the first American manned space program. According to the ascendant myth, astronauts were a new kind of hero, superpilots culled from the top rank of fighter jocks. Inside the ranks of these pilots, however, Wolfe learned different: a pilot who sat in a tiny capsule that he could not steer was, in the astronauts' private conversations, *Spam in a can*. By spending days and days with astronauts and their families, Wolfe became privy to this alternative narrative. His insider account felt intuitively true; and rather than knocking astronauts off their thrones, learning about the secret brotherhood of fighter jocks seemed to make most readers like them even more. Wolfe made them seem accessible and sympathetic.

Wolfe has such a singular, opinionated writing style that one might think *The Right Stuff* and his other nonfiction books were written in the first person. But as one moves through his cultural reporting to *Radical Chic & Mau-Mauing the Flak Catchers* (1970) and *Mauve Gloves & Madmen, Clutter & Vine* (1976) there is less and less of it. In his critiques of modern art (*The Painted Word*, 1975, and *From Bauhaus to Our House*, 1981), and in *The Right Stuff*, there is none.

Some of today's finest immersion writers have followed suit. John McPhee, Tracy Kidder, Adrian Nicole LeBlanc, and Katherine Boo all tend to keep themselves out of the story. Others, including me, use ourselves more, often as a character among many. Jon Krakauer, Sebastian Junger, Barbara Ehrenreich, Jeff Sharlet, Tony Horwitz, Lis Harris, and many others have often used the first person throughout.

But that doesn't mean these books are about *us*. In immersion journalism, there is always a subject beyond the narrator herself, something the writer sets out to investigate. Immersion writers may draw on their own experience (often they contrive it as a form of research) but they focus on the larger world. Personal experience, of course, is also the well from which memoir writers drink. But the difference between them and the writers I've mentioned above is clear and, to my mind, fairly stark: classic memoir is about what happened to me more than what I actively investigated so that I could write about it. Of course, in recent years the field of memoir has boomed, and now includes many accounts not just of life-as-it-happened-to-me, but life-as-I-made-it-happen. Elizabeth Gilbert famously visited Italy, India, and Indonesia for *Eat, Pray, Love*, and we do learn about those places in her book. But the real subject is her recovery from divorce. That's what makes *Eat, Pray, Love* a memoir. Barbara Ehrenreich's *Nickel and Dimed*, on the other hand, has relatively skeletal elements of what could be called a writer's journey of self-discovery. Ehrenreich, using herself as a guinea pig, set out to explore life as a minimum wage earner in the United States. Her own experience is Exhibit A, but her focus is always outwards—on her fellow waitresses and housekeepers, for example—instead of inwards. This is immersion writing.

Immersion in other cultures can take many forms. College students on a year abroad are immersing—especially if they don't spend too much time with others just like themselves. My first long trip to Mexico, with a group from my high school, lasted three weeks; most of my memories are of my American fellow-travelers. A homestay in Guadalajara was the heart of it; two classmates and I lived in a house belonging to a 50-something widow. Though we tried speaking Spanish with her, mostly we spoke to ourselves . . . in English. The experience was fun but didn't teach me nearly as much as a longer program in Spain the next summer, where each student lived with a different family and we didn't see our classmates every day. Both were like intro courses compared to when, two years into college, I returned alone to the town in Spain, worked a job in the local sausage factory, and took up with the young woman who had been my sweetheart two summers before.

The idea of immersion implies leaving home—or at least spending significant amounts of time outside it—engaged in daily exposure to your subjects and the problems they face. Writing that proceeds from this can answer complaints about the superficiality of journalism. It offers cures on several levels, one of which is the level of commitment. Immersion tells the reader: This is no drive-by. I did more than get a quote. I lingered and I listened. I got to know them as multidimensional. I probably know even more—often much more—than I have written. This reporting is authoritative. And this reporter can be viewed as a bearer of commitments, first to his subject and second to his craft.

Another benefit of immersion writing is empathy. It is hard to spend a lot of time with people without relating to them not just as sources but as human beings. The writer cannot help but come to appreciate the other's point of view, hopefully in a way that is both visceral and nuanced. This gives the writer's voice humanity, and makes the telling more compelling—and accessible.

Though "hanging out" may sound easy, the extended, deliberate, and thoughtful hanging out that we call immersion is difficult. Most of us can tolerate anyone for a half hour, but an entire day? Several days? Weeks and months? That's something else. The longer you go with a good subject, the more interesting it gets, and by interesting I don't necessarily mean pleasant: hanging around with drunken English soccer hooligans, as Bill Buford learned in *Among the Thugs*, can feel downright frightening. Being away from one's own kind can make a person homesick. But if I choose to write about it in the first person and I approach the task judiciously, the payoffs can be great: I become a sympathetic narrator, the reader's stand-in, the witness whose discomfort is felt vicariously. As with regular old bad news, the worse it gets, sometimes, the more interesting it becomes to read about.

vvv

What I call immersion writing has as recent ancestors all of the books I've mentioned so far. But its DNA goes back further than that, and some of it is shared with cousins that immersion writers sometimes acknowledge as family members, but other times pretend not to know.

I happened upon one of these cousins, ethnography, early in college, when I took an introductory anthropology class. I loved the course. It had some of the mind-bending aspects of philosophy, with a difference: instead of examining the thoughts of European men of letters, it was concerned with how diverse peoples from all over the world understand life, one goal being a profounder understanding of ourselves. Its classical form of research was to immerse oneself in a foreign place and make sense of it.

Field work reminded me of the reporting I'd done as a journalist, only it went deeper: it took longer, was harder, and was predicated on the idea that even "unimportant" people were worth talking to. It seemed potentially more meaningful to me.

My professor assigned us to read some classic ethnography—the description of cultures that results from this field work. Ethnographies can be about practically any aspect of our lives as social beings, and traditionally they described preliterate cultures in remote places. More recently, they have examined aspects of contemporary subcultures, from blues bars and drag shows to drug addicts and flight attendants, from corporations to animal shelters. I found many of these studies enthralling, took more anthropology courses, and read more ethnographies. Usually they melded description with analysis; I learned about ritual gift-giving in the South Pacific, ritual warfare in the Amazon basin, possible reasons that the consumption of pork is taboo for Jews and Muslims, how other cultures treat adolescents and sex, what rabbits might represent in folktales, how language reflects world-view, and more.

A pleasure for me was reading between the lines to try to understand what the immersion experience had been like for the ethnographer. The more recent ethnographies sometimes cast light on this; the classics generally do not. I wanted to know about the life of the researcher, voluntarily exiled from her culture for months or years, arriving unbidden like an alien and, in some cases, being treated like one.

Participant-observation, a term of art that grew up around ethnography to describe the process of involving oneself in a foreign culture, succinctly captured the tension and the drama of field work. One started on the outside, observing, taking in what one could from a distance: books, articles, films, language study, stories from others who had been there were all potentially of use.

And then one moved in. Where does participation really begin: on the dock, climbing off the boat? Upon first contact with the subject? Upon first entering his or her home? I think it begins when the investigator starts to bump up against the culture, and has to decide what she thinks about the taste of that soup, the feel of the rain, habits of greeting or the closeness of animals, gender roles and the sound of words. To me participant-observation is a process that can be represented reasonably well as a line with two poles:

observer → → → → → → → participant

From one's beginning as an observer, one moves along the scale, becoming incrementally more of a participant. You might think that finally arriving at that far pole is the measure of success, but in fact, for a professional, it would be a mark of failure, because it would mean you had come to totally identify with your subjects, and no longer identified with your colleagues or your own previous group. You had taken a local spouse, achieved fluency in the language, and instead of cringing at the sight of that monkey brain soufflé, you craved it. You had "gone native."

In other words, neither pole is where you want to be; it's the tension between them, the being partly in your group and partly outside, changed by the experience, thinking about them not purely as "them" but also to some degree as "us," that is fruitful intellectually (if not always comforting emotionally).

Ethnography and journalism are very different pursuits. Ethnography is long-term research into questions of human social life of particular interest to social scientists. Journalism is research (usually called "reporting") into issues of the day for a broad audience. I never received formal training in ethnography and don't feel that my journalism suffered as a result. But it appealed to me as a model in the ways it looked at people's lives and social worlds over time, just as the work of many celebrated journalists did. Sebastian Junger, author of *The Perfect Storm* and *War*, wrote his undergraduate thesis about Navajo long-distance runners (he ran with them). Anthropology, he told my class, "gave me a whole way of looking at the world" and "tools for understanding how humans interact with each other. . . . I've been mining it my whole life." Adrian Nicole LeBlanc, whose *Random Family: Love, Drugs, Trouble, and Coming of Age in the Bronx* tracked the lives of families over many years and is cited as an example by ethnographers, majored in sociology. Anne Fadiman, whose book *The Spirit Catches You and You Fall Down: A Hmong Child, Her American Doctors, and the Collision of Two Cultures* draws heavily on the work of ethnographers in describing the worldview of immigrants to California, values ethnographic insights but eschews any academic tone in her own writing, which is stylish and entertaining. Many top-rank nonfiction writers, among them Tracy Kidder, William Finnegan, Alex Kotlowitz, and Katherine Boo, believe in the payoffs of immersive, in-depth research that is essentially ethnographic without ever using the word.

I'll return to ethnography a bit in the chapters ahead—I found it helpful when it comes to thinking who to be/how to be in a research setting, what questions to ask, and other matters.

ᴠᴠᴠ

Another cousin of immersion writing is travel literature. By writing my first two books about my experiences with people on the move, I unwittingly became a sort of travel writer. I saw *Rolling Nowhere* and *Coyotes* shelved in the Travel section of many book stores, sometimes near guidebooks, sometimes near Paul Theroux or Peter Mayles' *A Year in Provence*. It was not what I expected (though I hadn't given classification much thought), but then again

... I entered a foreign world, dug in a bit, moved around, and recounted the experience in the first person: travel writing.

Non-touristic travel—that is, travel with a personal agenda, solo, and slow—has many intersections with immersion writing. Travel writing grew in the wake of European colonialism, and some of its best practitioners were uneasy representatives of empire such as Sir Richard Francis Burton. After being expelled from Oxford in 1842, Burton joined the army of the East India Company and, already skilled in languages, learned several more. Interested in local customs, he was considered an oddball by fellow officers, who dubbed him "the white nigger." In 1852, Burton gained the support of the Royal Geographical Society to explore Arabia. His secret agenda was to undertake a hajj to Mecca, and in 1853 he sailed for Cairo. There, disguised among other things as a Pathan from Afghanistan (to account for oddities in his self-presentation) and newly circumcised, Burton began the treacherous journey for which he is famous. His two-volume *Personal Narrative of a Pilgrimage to Al-Madinah and Meccah* is a foundational example of immersive travel writing, attentive to what today would be called culture (anthropology as a discipline was still in its infancy) and filled with adventure.

Employment with the British Raj also served the writerly development of George Orwell, who in 1922 took a posting with the Imperial Police in Burma (which Britain administered as a province of India) soon after graduation from Eton. His biographers have commented on how Orwell chafed under his responsibilities as a policeman—the locals hated him, and he hated the empire. Like Burton he had a reputation as an outsider, known for spending time alone and attending church services of the Karen ethnic group. Orwell returned to Britain in 1927, not only with dengue fever but with blue circle tattoos on each knuckle—a rural custom believed to protect against bullets and snake bites. The experience informed his first novel, *Burmese Days* (1934), and also the famous essay, "Shooting an Elephant" (1936). The moral quandaries posed by one's status in a foreign place, a rich potential vein in immersion stories, are front and center here when the narrator is called upon by locals to dispatch a rampaging elephant.

> And it was at this moment, as I stood there with the rifle in my hands, that I first grasped the hollowness, the futility of the white man's dominion in the East. Here was I, the white man with his gun, standing in front of the unarmed native crowd—seemingly the leading actor of the piece; but in reality I was only an absurd puppet pushed to and fro by the will of those yellow faces behind. I perceived in this moment that when the white man turns tyrant it is his own freedom that he destroys. He becomes a sort of hollow, posing dummy, the conventionalized figure of a sahib. For it is the condition of his rule that he shall spend his life in trying to impress the "natives," and so in every crisis he has got to do what the "natives" expect of him. He wears a mask, and his face grows to fit it.

Other great travel writers are more interested in capturing atmosphere, an idea of place—describing the Other in terms of the senses, historical echoes, and whatever else comes to mind. Jan Morris, Lawrence Durrell, and Bruce Chatwin are among them. Sometimes there's a personal story; sometimes the journey is a quest.

Travel writing is changing. The remote architectural treasures described by Robert Byron in *The Road to Oxiana* (1937) can be viewed on Wikipedia; intrepid retirees can visit most of them; and local people, with their camera phones and access to the Internet, today have a voice which in the past they did not. The world is full of new conversations, new people talking, and books no longer have such an exclusive franchise for introducing people to far-flung parts of the globe.

And yet the drama of one person encountering enveloping strangeness, and engaging other cultures, would seem to hold an enduring interest, and a lone narrator can still achieve in writing a precision and intimacy unavailable to those working in other media. To attract a reader the writing must be good and the experience on which it is based must be deep and sustained—in a word, immersive. Skimming the surface, simply visiting, won't cut it. Some tests of value: Are the writer's companions mainly fellow expats? Is there a local language that the writer does not speak and is not learning? Is the focus more on the writer's "personal journey" than on the people and places she finds herself?

A subgenre of travel writing that almost always passes these tests is the Peace Corps narrative. When President John F. Kennedy announced his creation of the Peace Corps on television in 1961, he probably didn't guess at the number of volunteers for whom the two-year experience in a foreign land would turn into literary material.

One reason it has is that the experience is almost always immersive gold: None of these writers was just passing through. And almost always they are there alone, in a faraway place with little connection to home; they need to connect with locals if they want a social life. Of necessity they eat what the local people eat, sleep where they sleep, etc.: it is almost like an ethnography corps.

Five books by Peace Corps volunteers—including two who didn't complete their stints—offer five strategies for successfully rendering the experience of two years in a faraway place.

One of the best is *River Town: Two Years on the Yangtze* (2001), by Peter Hessler. In it Hessler, a Princeton grad who had studied Chinese, is assigned to teach English and American literature in Fuling, a poor industrial city in Sichuan province. The town was a backwater; no American had lived there for 50 years. His workplace is the unprestigious Fuling Teachers College. Nevertheless, Hessler declares, "It was hard for me to imagine a better job. My students were eager and respectful, and they were bright"—at the time, in China less than two percent of the population was educated beyond high school.

> In fact I was glad to be at a lower-level school, because there was an unpolished quality to the students that I had never seen before. Everywhere else I had been, education ... was a game and students played it, but in Fuling they hadn't yet reached that point. Their intelligence was still raw—it smelled of the countryside, of sweat and muck, of night soil and ripening rapeseed and everything else that composed the Sichuanese farmland. And in their thoughts were flashes of the land, glimpses of the same sort of hard beauty that surrounded the teachers college, where the campus ended in terraced fields that ran steep up the side of Raise the Flag Mountain.

Hessler, challenged by his students, quotes their assignments and shares insights into their way of thinking at every opportunity. He understands that his workplace is an extension of the communist party, and politics comes up in everything: in what his students have to say about Robin Hood, in their textbooks' descriptions of Britain and America, in the way that "all of my students knew Marx; none of them knew Confucius." Hessler knows both, and encountering China with empathy and a touch of skepticism, he brings us in.

Working in a clinic in the Ivory Coast is a lot different from China, and Sarah Erdman's account of her two years there, *Nine Hills to Nambonkaha: Two Years in the Heart of an African Village* (2003), is different, too—more soulful, less boisterous. Of all these books, Erdman's conveys the most multifaceted experience of a village, and of her own difficult status there. Erdman has nothing to prove, and is perfectly willing to expose her own missteps. She wonders if what seems like her friendship with a village woman really is. Posted as a health worker who assists a government nurse, she's called on for help far from her expertise. But by reading from her *Birthing for Midwives* manual, she is able to assist a new mother whose placenta followed the baby out but whose umbilical cord is somehow still attached to the womb. On the other hand, she runs into trouble by treating a puppy she is given differently from the way other people do.

> Daouda appears in my courtyard one afternoon, strides right up to the puppy, and wallops him across the nose. I kick him out. Hitting the dog has been explicitly forbidden. He's outraged, but he knows he's done wrong; he shows up at night anyway [for a scheduled reading lesson]. But I am exhausted and my head throbs. I say to the boys outside the screen, I'm sorry, but could you please leave? . . . [They don't.]

Finally she just yells, in English, "Can't you just go home!" Everyone hushes. Their pride is wounded. Atoning for the outburst takes her days. I'm sure I'm not the first reader to think, *but I probably would have reacted the same way she did* . . . and this is exactly what first-person narration hopes to achieve.

Also engaging is Kris Holloway's *Monique and the Mango Rains: Two Years with a Midwife in Mali* (2006). Holloway's is stripped down, devoid of some of the sense-of-place detail that Erdman uses to take readers on a writerly journey. Instead, Holloway keeps a tight focus on her host and coworker, Monique Dembele, a village midwife whose job also involves her in life and death on a daily basis. The result is an account very much centered on the question of women's health, and the social forces that appear to converge to keep women pregnant, poor, and unhealthy. Holloway is a straightforward, no-nonsense narrator nevertheless capable of brief passages that pack a wallop:

> I remembered her. She was big in a dilapidated way. Her large head housed watery eyes, and her once mighty arms dangled in great bags from her bones. I sat beside her, gave her kola nuts, and drank millet beer out of her calabash. I shook her right hand, unaware that it had carved out girls' genitals for a living.

Set nearby in Togo but utterly different is *The Village of Waiting* (1984), by George Packer. Unlike Erdman and Holloway, Packer doesn't really love it there. When people persist in calling him *yovo*, or white person, a version of which happens to everyone in these books, he gets a bit irritated. He's assigned to teach English in the local school, but there are few scenes of him actually doing that, and we don't really come to know his students. He has quickly learned some Ewé, the local language, but it doesn't seem to help him bond too deeply with the villagers; we meet several who are likable, but none seem important to him. An extended saga involves Packer's realization that his apartment is being entered and items pilfered; eventually he catches the thief and denounces him to the chief, who is reluctant to take action but, under pressure, puts the young man on trial.

What Packer excels at is thinking about the larger picture. In the book's second sentence, we learn he has graduated from Yale; somehow it is not surprising that he does not think much of African pedagogy. Like other volunteers, he's a bit dismayed by the authoritarian style of his fellow teachers, but unlike them he takes his critique further. The local school, he writes, with its imported, sterile remnants of colonial education, its anger and humiliation, its bureaucracy and its whips, was a place where everyone was bound to fail, where failure was built in. Africans dressed up as dumb blacks imitating whites were made to see their own inadequacy. It had served the old need of the European colonizer to feel his superiority and importance; it served the need of the independent regime to preside over what it called "development" without losing power. Even under a black government, contempt for the black man hadn't been forgotten.

Instead of accepting as a given that the volunteer work is worth doing, Packer analyzes its efficacy, coming to feel that volunteers like himself are probably not making much of a difference in the big scheme of things. He feels frustrated to think that his legacy is more likely to be "a few concrete slabs, a couple of fuel-saving clay stoves, children who could speak some English." A section in the final third of the book begins, "I began my second year of teaching with a keen sense of irrelevance." He will leave before that year is over.

Packer, like Hessler, eventually made the transition from Peace Corps to staff writer for the New Yorker, where he often writes about politics and world affairs. His thoughtful early book shows that you don't need to write about success; trouble can be interesting.

The idea of unfinished business informs an introductory "Author's Note" to Tom Bissell's Chasing the Sea: Lost among the Ghosts of Empire in Central Asia.

I have never regretted leaving Uzbekistan. In fact, I soon profited by doing so, lucking in to a position at a New York publishing firm—a world that would, for most of my twenties, become my career. My premature departure from Uzbekistan [7 months into a 26-month commitment] is, nonetheless, probably the single biggest failure of my life. It is with a peculiar convergence of emotion that one looks back upon a failure that, as it turns out, had no meaningfully negative *personal* consequences at all. It leads to a heart-nibbling sort of reflection that leaves one racked with a sense of inadequacy difficult to explain to oneself, much less anyone else.

Chasing the Sea is a hybrid post–Peace Corps memoir and literary travel adventure. A pretext, of sorts, for the travel is an assignment from *Harper's* magazine to report on the Aral Sea, whose virtual disappearance over the past 50 or so years, due to a water diversion project, is a man-made ecological catastrophe. Most of the book recounts what happens on his way there.

Bissell meets up in Tashkent with his goofy, slang-infected translator, Rustam, who addresses him as "dude" and "bro"; revisits his host family; and spends time with current Peace Corps volunteers. His travels offer a bit of Robert Byron-esque architectural appreciation, ongoing dashes of the New Journalism (Rustam is used to good advantage), moving pieces of memoir. (Bissell is taken aback when his host mom shows him photos she kept of the girlfriend he was missing, and with whom he broke up after returning home. "Are you married?" she asks. "Where is your ring?") It is consistently witty, original, and entertaining. "Kamran was driving at a speed I would approximate at 310 miles per hour." "The driver Rustam dredged up . . . looked drunk, possibly stoned. His wall-eyed gaze seemed fixed upon the coast of some other compelling dimension." The final line of the acknowledgments section reads, "Thanks to Imodium A-D."

Bissell's and Packer's failures to fulfill their two-year commitment to the Peace Corps make their books, if anything, more interesting; failure doesn't have to mean failure. *Chasing the Sea* reminds us that depth of insight is just one virtue of an immersive experience; others can include reactions to it, compensations for it, any of the uncategorizable fillips to inspired writing.

vvv

So there are some examples of what immersion writing can be. Before we go further, here are a couple of examples of what I think it is not.

One of those things has sometimes, lately, been called *immersive journalism*. It's an effort to "bring the news alive" using elements of 3D gaming and virtual reality, including headsets, to conjure a sense of you-are-there, often with high definition audio and video, and the ability for the viewer to interact with content by changing perspectives—taking in a panoramic or 360-degree view by moving a smart phone, for example. It requires not only the talents of journalists but also the skills of computer and video production experts. The work interests me but it's not what I do. (Not yet, anyway!)

Nor do I include here projects where a writer concocts a conceit—say, attempting to live literally by the rules in the Bible for a year; live a year without buying things made in China; or spend a year reading the entire *Encyclopedia Britannica* or the *Oxford English Dictionary* (all have been done)—and recounts the lifestyle experiment for a book. I enjoyed sitting down with Joel Derfner as he researched *Swish: My Quest to Become the Gayest Person Ever and What Ended Up Happening Instead*, and I am pleased to be acquainted with Maria Dahvana Headley, author of *The Year of Yes*, about a woman who decides to say "yes" to every request for a date. (How could you not admire someone so willing to take such chances?) Some of these books transcend stunt to become decent memoir. But they are typically inquisitive in an inward direction; their goal is not to learn about the Other.

Memoir, speaking of, is another cousin to immersion writing. Memoirists tell a story about a lived experience, which immersion writers also do. But they put themselves front and center, and the experience that is their essential material is most often one through which they passed in the course of living their lives—not one they imagined in order to understand life for somebody else. That said, the first person voice, memoirists' stock-in-trade, can be used to great effect in immersion writing, and will be discussed throughout the book.

vvv

While writing up my experience on trains, I also applied for some graduate fellowships. I was awarded one that sent me to England for two years—or three, if I chose to stay on and pursue a doctorate. Several of my peers did, but that didn't feel right for me. The first copy of *Rolling Nowhere* arrived at school at the end of my first year, and got me thinking, *I want to do this again*.

I had an idea. While hopping freights I several times came across Mexican migrants doing the same thing. The American-born hoboes I was with tended to be scornful of the Mexicans, but it had occurred to me that in a certain way, they were the true modern-day inheritors of the American tramp tradition: immigrants traveling to work. The more I thought about it, the more I concluded that travel with Mexican migrants should be my next project.

Late summer of 1985 found me in the central Mexican state of Querétaro, trying to learn about what, from the locals' point of view, was *emigration* to my country. My host, a farmer, had traveled to the States in the 1960s to make money in the fields—the early part of a wave that expanded into the current century. Many, even most, of the men in the area, and growing numbers of women, had done the same thing. He heard me ask them about how they had managed the trip across the border, what it was like, had seen me fill notebooks with their replies. Finally he tired of hearing me ask the same old questions; I think he knew that I, afraid of the logical next step, was stalling. "It is better to see once than to listen many times," he said one day, as we left the house of his neighbor. For him the do-it-yourself step was familiar—something nervous-making to be sure, a thing of gravity, but nothing that half of his contemporaries hadn't themselves done already. For me it was unfamiliar and, from my point of view, risky in ways that his passage was not. My fair complexion would make me stand out, I would attract attention. Asking questions, I said to myself, was helping me prepare. But he'd had enough. Quit asking about it, he said in so many words, and just do it. Cross the border yourself. *Vaya*. Go.

That's good advice.

II. CHOOSING A SUBJECT AND GAINING ACCESS

Nobody can write the life of a man, but those who
have eat and drunk and lived in social intercourse with him.

SAMUEL JOHNSON, 1772

The calligrapher and her quills. The stone mason and his chisels. The floor finisher and his custom sanding machine. The violinist and her Strad/the jazz guitarist and her vintage Gibson. The bespoke tailor and his scissors.

If there were a major national magazine called, say, *Hand & Tool*, I would want to write for it. I'm fascinated by the relationships that develop between people with skilled callings and the tools that they appreciate more than anybody else. I loved the title of the bestseller from the '70s, *Zen and the Art of Motorcycle Maintenance*. I see a rich guy buying an expensive bicycle that he'll hardly ever ride and it hurts my heart. If you were the editor of *Hand & Tool* and we met at a party, I'd pitch you this story: people who work with meat rely heavily on their knives. The USDA beef inspectors I worked among at a Cargill Meat Solutions plant in Nebraska paid a huge amount of attention to the knives in their scabbards. All day long they cut into freshly slaughtered beef parts: heads, tongues, viscera, and big hanging sides headed on chains for the cool room. The work was hard on the arms, and if the blades were dull, it was much harder. Whenever they had a chance—including during the few seconds between when items passed on a chain or on a belt—they would hone their edges with a sharpening steel.

One of the inspectors, a native American named Terry, was universally acknowledged to be a Jedi master of the sharpening stone, and rescued me half a dozen times after my knife nicked a hook, a bone, or the steel table. In my mind, blades have an ancient, mystical quality, and everyone skilled at working them has a story to tell: Young King Arthur pulled a sword from a stone. My personal knife history began when my father, with great ceremony, handed me my first pocket knife the month before I went to summer camp, a coming-of-age ritual (*you need to be mature enough to handle a knife responsibly, and now I think you are*). What did Terry know about knives that his colleagues did not, and how did he learn it?

Alas, there is no such magazine as *Hand & Tool*. There is one called *Blade*, but it's focused almost purely on knives. The *New Yorker* once ran a long piece about a knife maker, which means they're likely done with the topic. Since I'm unable to imagine a good home for this piece, I will probably not write more about Terry than I have just now. Does that mean you should not write for your personal nonexistent magazine?

It's a question I can't really answer, because we all have our reasons for writing. Since writing, in most cases, will not make you rich, I'd say that the number one requirement of a topic is that it intrigue you. Anything less will not do, because this subject is likely to fill your brain for days, weeks, or months to come. And if the writer doesn't really care about it, the reader won't either.

BRAINSTORMING

When it comes to immersion writing, a good first question is this: what group of people interests you? Whose way of life have you always wanted to know more about? Whose outlook puzzles or annoys or intrigues you? Imagine the books and articles in your dream library: what would they be about? I'm talking about brain-

storming here, so don't just limit yourself to one publication—
describe, if you can, a small shelf of them. Think big and think
wide. *Wouldn't it be fascinating to . . . ?* or *Wouldn't it be amazing if . . . ?*
Then take the next step toward making your ideas real: write them
down.

A next question that a professional writer would consider is,
probably, which of these thoughts connects to the zeitgeist—to
what's in the news, what's on TV, what people are talking about;
and not just this week, but for the foreseeable future (because
good writing takes time). Topicality is not required of a good idea,
but it can help when it comes time to get published. An article
about Doctors Without Borders may attract more interest in a time
of epidemics. Writing about veterans may find more traction in a
time of war. Pieces about transsexuality, violence on campus, or
professional sports and injury/drugs/money all have their season.

Of course, if you're a student and publication matters less than
practice, then consider letting topicality fall by the wayside. Besides, for some projects, it really doesn't matter. When I decided
to ride the rails, hoboes certainly weren't in the news. (Home-
lessness was, but that was only peripherally related.) Obscurity
can even be intriguing. Nobody, I'd submit, appreciates this as
much as the writer Susan Orlean, who time after time pursues
off-beat, unprepossessing topics and makes them interesting. A
10-year-old boy in New Jersey, an independent grocery store in
Queens, New York, a guy in trouble for stealing orchids from a
Florida state park—Orlean's gift is in taking the ordinary and, by
the things she notices and the way she casts it, making it extraordinary.

More than once, Orlean has read something in the news that
piqued her interest in a related, non-newsy topic. After the bomb-
ing of the Alfred Murrah Federal Building in Oklahoma City in
1995, Orlean wrote me,

I was struck by the frequent mention that Tim McVeigh [one of the bombers] lived in a trailer park. It seemed like shorthand for something we all automatically understand, but what piqued my interest was that when I thought about it, I realized I had no idea at all of what living in a trailer park was like. I suspect if I had proposed a story about trailer parks without that gloss of topicality, it would have been a hard sell as a story (although the *New Yorker* is awfully generous that way). But having that connection, however tenuous, made the story feel anchored in the moment. I mentioned Oklahoma City in the story only once, in one sentence. And I certainly didn't pitch the story as one about Timothy McVeigh. But I do like burrowing into a topical story and finding the bit of it that I don't understand and using that as my story. Another example of this is the piece I did on children's beauty pageants. It came about because of the Jon Benet Ramsay murder—again, lots of mentions of her being a participant in them, but no explanation of what that actually *meant*. I hate the idea that we just assume we know a subculture when we really don't, so that's what inspires me to find stories that way.

A talented newspaper columnist I knew had an interest in Samoan-Americans that, after his second or third column about some in Denver, began to seem a bit eccentric. (Columnists and bloggers can often self-assign a topic; sometimes their ideas strike a chord, sometimes not.) Anne Fadiman's choice of Hmong immigrants in Merced, California, might seem similarly specific until you see how her focus—a Hmong girl whose epilepsy couldn't be effectively treated due to cultural misunderstandings with American doctors—illuminated a huge challenge in public health and the training of doctors. Fadiman's extraordinary book

The Spirit Catches You and You Fall Down, in print since 1998, has sold nearly a million copies.*

One might wonder about the market for a book about Mexico's Tarahumara Indians. But Christopher McDougall focused on the one thing they are famous for—long-distance running—and turned his engagement with them into an entertaining book, *Born to Run: A Hidden Tribe, Superathletes, and the Greatest Race the World Has Never Seen*. The fact that McDougall himself is an avid runner matters to the story, and suggests a good question for the prospective immersion writer to ask herself: is there a way in which my personal story resonates with this topic? If so, it opens up a world of possibility in terms of first-person narration.

Jon Krakauer's presence on a calamitous alpine expedition allowed him to write *Into Thin Air: A Personal Account of the Mount Everest Disaster*. The story was automatically exciting, but what made it satisfying to read was Krakauer's status as an experienced climber among relative newbies, which allowed him to consider bigger questions such as, *Would climbers have looked out for each other more if it weren't a commercial expedition? How does money change the ethic of backcountry adventure?*

Ideally your subject is either in the news or lurking right behind headlines and has an untold story: the bravery and stressful lives of soldiers in Afghanistan (Sebastian Junger, *War*), Hasidic Jews in Brooklyn (Lis Harris, *Holy Days*), small towns living with methamphetamine (Nick Reding, *Methland*). You might fit right into a local bowling league—but would anyone care? Ask yourself, could I explain why this matters to (a) a regular person, and (b) an editor in New York?

---

* I asked Anne Fadiman if she hadn't worried, over the several years it took her to report and write the book, that somebody else might beat her to it. Fadiman replied, "Not too many other writers were hot on the trail of a Hmong immigrant girl with epilepsy."

Sometimes, it helps to think of the larger question and then try to imagine a situation that might cast light on it. What's it like in those assisted living facilities that dot the land? Maybe I'll just move into the one where my mother lives for a while (Dudley Clendinen, *A Place Called Canterbury: Tales of the New Old Age in America*). Or get a job in one that specializes in Alzheimer's patients (Lauren Kessler, *Dancing with Rose*). Why is Civil War reenactment such a huge thing, 150 years after the fact? Maybe I could spend a little time with some hard-core reenactors and find out (Tony Horwitz, *Confederates in the Attic: Dispatches from the Unfinished Civil War*).

As these examples show, there are many ways to find a story. In every case, as you develop your idea, it will make sense to ask these two questions: *What's the story?* And, next, *What's the underlying story—the reason that this topic matters?* If you can draw a persuasive line between that rural bowling league and, say, America's obesity epidemic, or the aging of America's rural white communities, there might be hope for your idea. But one team's struggle to dominate the regional league? Susan Orlean might be able to make readers care, but other writers could have trouble.

Ideas come to each of us differently. In any case, coming up with a topic in immersion writing is only the first step. The next step is to put it to a test: is this a story I could actually get?

WAYS TO GET INSIDE

Access is a key question for immersion writing. After we imagine *who* we'd like to talk to, we come to the matter of *how*. It would be fascinating to learn about the dynamics of a polyamorous relationship, or to watch a hedge fund manager pick a stock. To listen in on a conclave of Grand Dragons of the Ku Klux Klan, or on the conversations between a doctor and a patient seeking gender reassignment, or on a group of children mustering the strength to stand up to a bully. All would be amazing. But how?

Access is the great spoiler of immersion wish lists. How are you going to get to know these people? Many groups, from Hell's Angels to anti-abortion activists, are not only uninterested in publicity, they may be actively averse to it.

Journalists bump into this question every day. The unanswered email, the unreturned phone call—it's very much business as usual. People have no obligation to talk to the press and may have good reasons for avoiding it. Sometimes *credentials* matter. If you're lucky enough to be able to say you're calling from the *New York Times* or CNN or NBC or National Public Radio, you may succeed more often. If you're Tom Wolfe, those astronauts are going to be more ready to talk to you. Sometimes the phrase "access journalism" has been used to refer to a practice of trading on relationships (and in certain circles a shady expectation of tit-for-tat) to arrange an interview with somebody famous or important.

That's not what I'm talking about here. Immersion writing is most often based on a different sort of access—access to regular folks. Lesser-known people can be easier to meet, and still have lives that are hugely interesting. Drug dealers' girlfriends (Adrian Nicole LeBlanc), the Amish (Joe Mackall), high school football players (H. G. Bissinger), rural Mormons (Jon Krakauer), students at a Christian university (Kevin Roose)—with patience and cleverness and possibly a friendly connection or two, a writer might get to know people like that. If it seemed worthwhile, he might become part of their world. That insight would be generated from this experience, and stories, is inevitable. Most of the writers mentioned in this book made their mark by seeking out worlds that the larger society understood only from surface impressions. Behind the shorthand and stereotypes that most people settled for, they saw depth.

But how did they do it? How can you? I've thought about access long and hard. It's often the prerequisite for what I hope to accomplish, the first step that there's no getting around. (In certain extreme situations like the ones I've pursued, it can literally take years—I spent much longer applying to become a correction officer and waiting for my number to be called than actually doing the job.) While it holds the potential for frustration, this part of a project is often the most creative and interesting, as you learn your way around a new world and make your first forays into it.

My first advice is to relax and take a few breaths. Arranging access is sometimes a matter of making a key phone call, but more often it seems to be a process of gradual discovery, something that unfolds over days, weeks, or months. That time is spent in learning not just about *how to get in* but also about the dimensions of your subject, what it is you might write about. In the course of interviewing New York State correction officers about their jobs before I ever applied myself, for example, I learned they had all gone through a seven-week training academy. *If they'd give me access as a journalist*, I thought to myself, *watching a session of that could make a great article*. As it happened, they denied me access ... but the training academy, once I became an officer myself, eventually became a chapter of my book. You're an explorer in a new world, and it naturally can take some time to gain your bearings.

Let's consider a range of scenarios for gaining access.

- *You already have a connection.*

Do you speak a foreign language? Were your grandparents refugees, were your parents Mennonites, is your aunt undergoing fertility treatments? Are you the adult child of an alcoholic? If so, you may already have an entree into a group that I wouldn't have. Consider using it.

- *You know somebody.*

Your boyfriend's dad is a tugboat pilot. Your mother, a lawyer, has an associate who represents a hacker collective. You once temped at a collection agency. Each of these situations represents a potentially interesting story and a person who might vouch for you or make an inquiry on your behalf. Consider using them.

To get started on a project investigating right-wing political power in Washington, DC, the writer Jeff Sharlet contacted the brother of a former girlfriend, who was connected to that world. The query eventually mushroomed into an article for *Harper's* and his book, *The Family: The Secret Fundamentalism at the Heart of American Power*, which he researched by living at a residence for conservative Christians in Arlington, Virginia.

Anne Fadiman got the idea for *The Spirit Catches You and You Fall Down* from a college friend who was a doctor in California's Central Valley, where the story takes place. By introducing her to colleagues, he helped her gain a toehold in a story (which later entailed all kinds of other access challenges).

I wanted to write about the chaotic traffic and unplanned urban growth of Lagos, Nigeria, for my book *The Routes of Man*. But I didn't know a soul in Lagos. Or did I? I vaguely remembered that I'd bought life insurance from a Nigerian immigrant (long story) back when I began working as a correction officer. It took me a while to track down Agbonifo Akpata; he had moved on to real estate management. But he not only remembered me (I was the only person who had responded to his mass mailing), he immediately offered to arrange for a trusted driver to pick me up at Lagos' notorious international airport, and later I was able to stay with relatives of his in a working class Lagosian neighborhood.

Be aware, though, of a possible pitfall about finding a story through a friend: in terms of your ability to ask the questions you need to ask and tell the story in the way it needs to be told, will that connection tie your hands? In my experience, you almost certainly do not want to write *about* a friend, if that friend is still alive:

you will feel too constrained.[†] And, if the piece you're working on involves anything potentially sensitive, you want to be cautious about making your subject the friend of a friend, as well.[‡]

• *There's a nonprofit group, or NGO, that might help.*

Often, when you're writing about an area of social concern, there is a nonprofit group already at work on it. If your interests dovetail, they might agree to help you out. One such organization, the Arizona Farmworkers' Union, helped me meet migrants for my second book, *Coyotes*. Another, The Orphan Project in New York City, intrigued me just with its name; a short item I read in the paper, early in the AIDS epidemic, explained that its founder was concerned that a wave of orphans would follow the spread of the disease into populations of people with children. When I spoke with her, she told me about how some adoption agencies were trying to match adoptive parents to children of people with AIDS who had not died yet, so that they might participate in planning for the care of their kids. After I pitched the story to the *New York Times Magazine* and got an assignment, one of the agencies agreed to help me find a parent going through the process; I followed the story for almost a year in order to write "The Hand-Off."

• *You find access via a business.*

This can work, if you can get past most companies' hesitance to accommodate publicity that's not under their control. I received

---

[†] For an example of friendship used to honor and make sense of a death, I recommend *The Short and Tragic Life of Robert Peace*, by Jeff Hobbs.

[‡] And speaking of wariness over writing about friends: in Aspen, in 1989, I asked Hunter S. Thompson why he had never written about his adopted home. (Thompson had run for sheriff there in 1970 on a pro-drug platform, narrowly losing, and had strong opinions about the way the town was changing.) "That's easy," he said. "You don't shit in your own nest."

permission from a Belgian-owned trucking company in Kenya to travel with its drivers into Central Africa; they understood that my goal was to get to know them in the context of the AIDS epidemic. Likewise I was given permission by a Peruvian transport firm to accompany its drivers from Lima to Cuzco, and then from Cuzco down into the rainforest. In both cases I was working on assignment from magazines (the *New Yorker* and *National Geographic*). Nicholas Dawidoff spent a year with the New York Jets to write *Collision Low Crossers: A Year Inside the Turbulent World of NFL Football*, an immersive account that focuses on coaching and the back office. That echoed the permission gained by George Plimpton to play briefly on professional sports teams, including the Detroit Lions football team and the Boston Bruins hockey team. The writer Bob Reiss spent several months inside Delta Air Lines to gain context for a book about a single 72-hour, 9-stop, 15,000-mile outing on one plane (*Frequent Flyer: One Plane, One Passenger, and the Spectacular Feat of Commercial Flight*). In each case, the writer's reputation was no doubt key to securing the assignment; no management team would okay a project that carried obvious risk to the company's reputation. (Here it's important to remember, however, that any writer who promises favorable treatment in advance, or offers a subject the right to review and reject a manuscript ahead of publication, is engaged not in journalism but in *public relations*.)

- *There's a connection you could pay for.*

Money can make a difference, and it's usually professionals who have it. Documentary filmmakers often use fixers to introduce them to the right people, help with transportation logistics, etc. Journalists working overseas sometimes hire a local person to translate for them, or, again, for introductions. It is a timeworn strategy that, as a freelance, I had never considered until I landed that assignment from *National Geographic* to report on a new cross-continental highway in Peru. The assigning editor asked me for a list of expenses and then remarked on the absence of a budget line for a "fixer." The more I thought about it, the more I understood the potential usefulness of such a person, particularly when you're working on a deadline. On my second trip to Peru, to do additional research for *The Routes of Man*, I hired a young Canadian living in Peru who had been the assistant to the *National Geographic* photographer on the first trip. Tim Currie was great company, and provided a measure of security, I felt, when we ventured deep into the rainforest to an area where mahogany was logged illegally. In that case, one fixer led to another: a boatman we hired, whom Tim had worked with before, used his connections to get us into a remote encampment where the loggers lived so that we could witness the deed being done.

Publications might pay for a trip with an adventure travel company, as *Travel + Leisure* magazine did a couple of times for me; my job was to then write about the group experience. Or, in a more extreme situation, you could pay for and document a very un-leisurely type of group travel, as writer Luke Mogelson and photographer Joel van Houdt did when they bought passage on a smuggler's boat carrying undocumented migrants from Indonesia to Australia's Christmas Island, and recorded the voyage for the *New York Times Magazine*.§

§ Paying subjects directly for their stories has long been considered verboten in journalism, the concern being that it can corrupt the reporting process. But the extended voluntary participation of subjects in a long article or book does raise the question, *shouldn't there be a way for them to share in profits?* Jon Krakauer, in Robert Boynton's *The New New Journalism*, describes how he paid one of the subjects in his book *Under the Banner of Heaven* $20,000 in exchange for the right to quote from her unpublished memoir. He recounts defending this to a group of journalists: "I've made a boatload of money off of the books I've written. Don't you think I owe anything to some of my subjects, who got

- *You improvise access over time.*

Some of the most compelling literary immersions of our time have developed piecemeal, the writers beginning with one story that evolved into another. Adrian Nicole LeBlanc was following the criminal trial of a heroin dealer known as Boy George when she made the acquaintance of Jessica, one of his girlfriends. Once the kingpin was convicted and sent away, LeBlanc continued following the lives of Jessica and other women in her circle—for more than 10 years! They had babies, relationships with other men, and their own prison terms while LeBlanc, always listening, always there or a phone call away, remained their Boswell. *Random Family* is a landmark work of immersive narrative nonfiction.

Alex Kotlowitz, then a staffer for the *Wall Street Journal* in his adopted home of Chicago, had been hanging out around West Side housing projects, looking for stories, when a photographer invited him along as he took portraits of some kids; Kotlowitz would write the text for a photo essay. Among the kids were Pharoah and Lafeyette Rivers, then 7 and 10 years old. Kotlowitz, suspecting that just the everyday facts of their lives in the violence-plagued projects would make a good newspaper article, met their mother, LaJoe, started spending time with the family, and wrote an article for the *Journal* that was well received. He decided to extend the project, following the boys for over two years. The title for his book *There Are No Children Here* is a quote from their mom, who was making the point that the projects are so violent that children quickly lose their innocence, and sometimes their lives.

A quieter book is Joe Mackall's *Plain Secrets: An Outsider among the Amish*. A writing instructor at a college in rural Ohio, Mackall lives in a community with many Amish and over time, he got to know

---

nothing for the crucial assistance they provided except, in some instances, unwanted publicity?"

his closest Amish neighbors, the Shetler family. The long, gradual process took a leap forward when the father, Samuel, accepted Mackall's offer to drive him up to his mother's funeral in Canada (the Shetlers had only a horse and buggy for transportation). Mackall's firsthand narration is enhanced by his extensive reading in literature *about* the Amish, and particularly about the austere sect to which the Shelter family belongs, known as Swartzentruber Amish.

Alice Goffman's book, *On the Run: Fugitive Life in an American City*, is a bit of an outlier here; Goffman wrote not narrative nonfiction but a sociological study of young black men in Philadelphia. Still, her ethnographic research might easily have been used in the service of a trade nonfiction book. With examples that are startling and fresh, Goffman, who is white, painted a picture of how the means of advancement, mainly illegal, that are available to the men also alienate them from social institutions from health care to family life, and give the police tremendous power over their lives. Goffman's entree was gradual: At first, by working in a university food service, she mainly got to know African American women. But as her acquaintances deepened, she wrote, she was most profoundly struck by the situation of the young men whose lives many of the women's rotated around. She moved off-campus and followed the men over several years as they shot others, got shot themselves, got arrested, relocated, and regrouped.

Other writers whose access was gradual and evolving include Stanley Booth (*Dance with the Devil: The Rolling Stones and Their Times*), Bill Buford (*Among the Thugs*), Nick Reding (*Methland: The Death and Life of an American Small Town*), and Jen Percy (*Demon Camp: A Soldier's Exorcism*).

I'd be remiss to close a discussion of access without also crediting the role of animal cunning. One of Tom Wolfe's great access coups was attending a cocktail party thrown for members of the

Black Panther party by Leonard Bernstein, at the composer's elegant duplex on Park Avenue. This meeting of liberals and revolutionaries is the subject of his famous article "Radical Chic: That Party at Lenny's." Wolfe, spotting an invitation for the affair atop the unattended desk of David Halberstam one day while visiting *Harper's* magazine, told Nieman Storyboard that he called the RSVP number, gave them his name, and told them he accepted. His name was on the list at the door.

- *You go undercover.*

I doubt too many people worry about the ethics of sneaking into a fancy party, as Wolfe did. In other contexts, though, surreptitious access—into an institution, a political movement, a criminal organization—would probably be considered "going undercover." The decision to go undercover needs to be considered very carefully. It is an approach that should be used sparingly, and only when the topic is of sufficient gravity to justify its many risks. It opens up a Pandora's box of ethical concerns, can lead to feelings of anger and betrayal on the part of subjects, and typically places the researcher in a position of emotional and spiritual duress, as well. That said, it can be a powerful investigative tool, exciting and illuminating. I have devoted chapter IV to undercover reporting, including the questions around deceptive access.

Access will ultimately depend on an interaction between *you* and *them*. On the *you* side of the equation are these factors: how you present yourself in style (Do you sound confident? friendly? sincere?) and in substance (Have you done your homework? Are you asking about something this person is knowledgeable about?). On the *them* side, for anyone weighing your overture, are questions such as these: *Is this a serious person? Where are they coming from? Will talking to him help me or my organization? Do I have time to speak or email with her? Or, most baldly, what's in it for me?*

My students often need to recalibrate expectations when it comes to access. Saying you are a student of journalism, for example, is not much of a credential. It is unlikely to impress many important people.

On the other hand, a surprising number of people are interested in publicity—or in simply talking to somebody—and are perfectly willing to give of their time "on spec" (in other words, even if the caller does not have an assignment). Among the most willing are often activists, campaigning politicians, partners opening a new restaurant (or others involved in an array of startups), and creative people (actors, artists, comedians, writers, chefs) on their way up. My most successful student writers often leverage friendships they already have, using their acquaintances as subjects or as conduits to subjects. Among them have been volunteers involved in animal rescue, drag queens, Christians involved in "seeding" new churches, recovering addicts, young athletes, Wiccans, coffee experts including those involved in barista competitions, sex workers, halal chicken cart vendors, and young male gamers (from Warhammer to speedrunning). Other students have succeeded simply by emailing (the leader of a group of female drone enthusiasts), calling (a member of a cave exploration club), or attending a meet-up posted online (of a shy people's support group).

Credentials may matter—but also they may not. If I'm approached for an interview by someone from a website I've heard of who knows little about my work, and someone from a lesser-known site who has done her homework and has questions that interest me, and I only have time for one interview, I might opt for the latter. So preparation can matter. As can personality, attitude, and the way you present yourself. An undergraduate proposed to me a profile of an entrepreneur whom she knew slightly and felt would sit for a long interview with her. I worried she might have unrealistic expectations, but she assured me I was wrong. "Is he a family friend?" I pressed. No, she said. "Then why will he spend this much time with you?" She shrugged. "Pretty girl?" she predicted. (She got the interview.) Cold-calling (or cold-emailing or Facebook messaging) is tough; it's hard when so much is riding on a first impression. Don't sell yourself short by muttering or acting as though you expect anything other than a *yes*—assume a confident pose (even if you don't *feel* confident), cheerfully wag your tail, and people—*some* people, at any rate—will respond in kind.

III. ONCE INSIDE

Of every hue and caste am I, of every rank and religion,
A farmer, mechanic, artist, gentleman, sailor, quaker,
Prisoner, fancy-man, rowdy, lawyer, physician, priest.
I resist every thing better than my own diversity.
WALT WHITMAN, "Song of Myself"

Journalism is the only occupation in which at all times
you know less than anyone else in the room.
ADRIAN NICOLE LEBLANC

A mariner's story. Do I believe it?
Verily, I do not care. There is no lie that
does not have at its core some truth.
One must only know how to listen.
J. M. COETZEE, *Age of Iron*

US & THEM
Self-Presentation and "Who To Be"

A writer came up to me recently after I gave a talk and asked, "When you do these immersions, can you be yourself?"

Yes, I said. Yes, because who can you be besides yourself?

I'd venture that fairly few people, even the most honest and forthright, present themselves exactly the same to everyone they meet during the day. I am somebody a little different to each of them. To my daughter, I'm Daddy. To some of my students, I'm "Professor"; to others, I'm "Ted." To strangers emailing me for the first time, I'm sometimes "Mr. Conover." To the policeman pulling me over for running a stop sign, I might be "Sir," even if the respectful address is a prelude to giving me a ticket. I speak differently to my mother than to a cocktail waitress. And each of them, in turn, sees a different person when they look at me.

Are we "acting" when we speak differently to different people? The idea of inhabiting different roles as we pass through life was certainly familiar to William Shakespeare. His famous "all the world's a stage" monologue considers how our roles in life's drama change as we age: we go from helpless infant to whining schoolboy, then lover, then soldier, then smug and vain and, finally, incapacitated and helpless again.

The sociologist Erving Goffman (the father of Alice) applied the theater metaphor to our daily existence in his seminal book, *The Presentation of Self in Everyday Life*. Not only do we act out roles as we move through life, he suggested, but often we choose our stage, our props, and our costumes. We strive to make different impressions on different people and present ourselves to best advantage in different settings, all the while aware that others are taking our measure. Each person's performance is her own, of course, but its contexts are situations with rules and expectations that we've all agreed upon: a classroom, a doctor's office, a sporting event, a dinner party, all come with implicit scripts, ways we're supposed to behave. Typically, the players are invested in having a successful performance, in maintaining decorum; he quotes Simone de Beauvoir on the crisis that ensues when accidents knock askew a mask: "Wine is spilled on her dress, a cigarette burns it; this marks the disappearance of the luxurious and festive creature who bore herself with smiling pride in the ballroom."

When a researcher asks herself, *Will I be able to pass?*, she can thus be understood to be worrying about her incomplete knowledge of the rules and expectations of a particular drama.* Preparation can be a partial cure, but since real life requires extemporaneous performance, it's not enough.

So back to the question, *Can I be myself?* A better answer is probably, *It's best if you are.* Because it's difficult to be somebody you are not, especially over the long term. It's difficult to lie, especially to lie a lot, and not get caught at it. It's difficult to establish rapport, I think, if you do not exude a sense of authenticity, of feeling comfortable in your skin. When I am living like somebody else for a while, which is my version of undercover, I try to fit in not by *adding* false information about myself (like a fake backstory, which I'll need to remember and which I might be tempted to elaborate on in a weak moment), but rather by *subtracting*—by not mentioning facts about myself which are inconvenient, which could give me away. It's safer and to me it feels better.

For example: as a new correction officer, why shouldn't I tell my colleagues that I'm married and have young kids? Doing so might help to explain why I look tired, why I'm not interested in working double shifts. Further, it might prompt fellow officers to tell me a bit about *their* families, and that's all for the good. The same when I worked as a federal meat inspector in Schuyler, Nebraska. People were curious when I showed up in town solo, and those I became friendly with would ask about why I'd left the East Coast. My answers were all true: I grew up in Colorado, and had been missing this part of the country. You can get enough of New York City. I got tired of paying a small fortune for a small apartment. My son went

---

* Students arriving at a selective college for their freshman year may experience this same kind of anxiety, wondering, for example, whether the institution made a mistake in accepting them, whether they'll be exposed as frauds.

off to college and I wasn't tied to home anymore. My wife said she didn't mind; I'll probably see her before long.

Where it gets more complicated is when you meet somebody you like and start getting to know each other better. The meat inspector who trained me, Stan, knew I hadn't qualified for the job by having experience, as he had, and deduced that I must have gone to college, the other way to get an inspector job. He asked me that very question one day on the "heads" line, during the five- or six-second pause we had between cutting into the giant skinned cow heads that passed in front of us, dripping blood as they dangled from hooks.

"Yeah, I went to college," I told him. As the next pause in our labor arrived, he asked the follow-up question: "So where'd you go?"

That one I didn't want to answer: on the off-chance he had heard of Amherst College and knew it was an elite institution, all kinds of uncomfortable questions might start passing through his mind. So I replied, simply, "I think I'd rather not talk about it."

I worried that he'd fault me for being secretive. Instead, he later told me he respected me for it, that all the people he knew who'd been to college wouldn't stop talking about it.

Back to Sing Sing: law enforcement jobs may make it easier to be secretive, because there's a kind of cop who's not that keen on talking about himself. (In addition, at the corrections academy, we'd been told not to share personal information about ourselves at work, in case inmates might overhear it and use it against us.) I became that kind of non-self-disclosing officer, or thought I did. The first evidence I had of personality leakage, you might call it, was on Halloween. The officer-in-charge of B-block, the gigantic cellblock where I'd been working for several months, was an attractive African-American woman a few years younger than me. We knew each other's names but hadn't exchanged more than greetings on the dozen or so occasions when our paths crossed. Still, at shift's end, as a handful of us were standing around before heading home and Halloween plans were being discussed, the woman said, "How about you, Conover? Where you gonna be tonight?" As I started to say I'd probably go out trick-or-treating with my kids, she interrupted: "I see you maybe headin' down to the Village, I don't know why." I don't think she was insinuating anything about me with that; I just think I gave off some vibe that she picked up—in years past I had indeed spent Halloween in Greenwich Village, and worked there during the day, too.

Rapport

The best immersive researchers are probably those attentive to social cues, people who are reasonably social and reasonably self-aware. My operating philosophy is that many people are frightened of strangers, so the first thing you want to be is nonthreatening. You want to try to fit in. If you are young and have body piercings and tattoos and hope to sit in on a meeting of your great aunt's chapter of the Daughters of the American Revolution, consider leaving studs and hoops at home and covering some of your skin. If you want to speak to the squatters out by the freight yards, don't wear expensive jewelry. A more "normal" appearance may be more versatile than a more "extreme" appearance, though I'm sure there are endless exceptions. If you are a man who wears makeup, for example, you may have greater access to the world of men who wear makeup than I would. Accent, diction, and word choice can set you apart (though George Plimpton, with his plummy accent, didn't let that stop him). If building rapport is high on your list of research objectives, as I believe it must be, you must naturally ask yourself, *Is there anything about me they're not going to like?* When people look at me will they see, at least to some degree, themselves? If we are unwilling or unable to change the way we present, it may suggest we are unsuited to research among certain kinds of people.

Or it may not. There are workarounds. Truman Capote, known for his fiction, wanted to learn about life in the small Kansas town of Holcomb, and wanted to speak to people there about the terrible murder of a farm family, the Clutters. Capote, however, had a gay affect that he perhaps rightly assumed might not "play well" in a Midwestern small town; and indeed, as his biographer Gerald Clarke wrote, "Inevitably he was greeted with derision" in Holcomb. But Capote had had the foresight to ask his childhood friend, the writer Harper Lee, to accompany him. Lee, who presented as more "normal," was good at meeting strangers, establishing a toehold, and then introducing them to her friend Truman. In other words, Capote secured access in part through the introductions of a skillful intermediary. (For the kind of research he conducted in order to write In Cold Blood, a series of lengthy interviews was sufficient. But for an immersive account of everyday life in Holcomb, it might not have been; I have difficulty imagining Capote fitting in at a meeting of the local Grange or Rotary, at Sunday church services, etc.[†])

Approaching Mexican workers in Arizona, I probably stood out as much as Capote had in Kansas. But I was introduced to them by Lupe Sanchez, the Mexican-born director of a farmworkers group, whom they appeared to trust completely. Sanchez also made a great suggestion to me: *offer them English classes.* His introduction, those classes I taught, and the passage of time all helped me to "be myself" and enjoy the company of those workers. And the sugges-

---

[†] For a bold, good-humored account of a dark-skinned writer breaching ethnic barriers, see *Searching for Whitopia: An Improbable Journey to the Heart of White America* (2009), by Rich Benjamin.

tion that I offer English classes morphed into a useful question that I've asked myself innumerable times since: How can I be of use? Can I teach, babysit, make a meal, offer a ride? Traditionalists might object to these suggestions, believing that the exchange of anything besides information can compromise fairness. They are right, to a point: gifts and freebies can chase away the truth. But that strict line makes the most sense in traditional reporting situations. In immersion writing, sources are often giving writers a great deal of their time, with no clear promise of anything in return. The least a writer can do, in a situation like that, is to offer to help out—in simple ways that won't unduly complicate a relationship. In other words, I don't believe a writer should offer to hold the bag of drugs, or loan money, or massage that sore shoulder. But if a writer can help with the kids' homework, do a little babysitting, pay for the takeout food, or mind the shop briefly while the source takes a break, I think she should consider it.

The main reason I think people allow me to spend time with them, though, is that they see I will listen. I find them interesting; I want to know how they do things, I want to learn their opinions on a wide range of topics. In my experience, people want to tell their story.

Note that this differs from the posture of other kinds of professional investigators, be they in law enforcement or science. I don't want to come off as a person trying to impress sources with my degree or my authority. Rather, since they are the ones who know what I want to learn, it makes sense to look at them as my teachers. I then become the devoted student, who wants to know everything. I am there not to judge but to learn.

By the same token, I should add that I don't think that building rapport means laughing along at inappropriate jokes or saying (or agreeing with) things I don't believe. You need to be yourself, and if you are not a racist, then don't laugh at the racist joke. Smile knowingly and commit the joke to memory so that you can put it in your notes later.

How to Think about Yourself

Anybody 19 years old who has tried to order alcohol in a bar where you have to be 21 knows about trying to affect a confident pose. And many (often with the help of a fake ID) have pulled it off.

But an even better way to succeed is to achieve true comfort inside your own skin. If you're in an uncomfortable situation, this could take some time. I had been riding the rails for nearly a month when I arrived in Havre, Montana, a small town with a large train yard. It was said to have an extensive "jungle," or hobo campground, but I couldn't find it. As I walked I heard a banging sound inside the yard; expecting a railroad crew, I was surprised to come upon a guy about my age, hacking away with a hatchet at some wooden bracing around the edge of a freight car. He pointed me toward the jungle and explained that he needed some wood for his campfire there. Then, as I wrote in *Rolling Nowhere*, he looked at me more closely.

"Hey," he asked. "You a tramp?"

"What?"

"I said, 'Are you a tramp?'"

Few questions could have caught me so off guard. I was prepared to answer almost any question a tramp might ask of me as though I were a tramp, but this struck right at the heart of the matter. I gulped and looked back at him as though he were crazy—a good way, I figured, to defend the length of my pause.

"Yeah," I answered, too defensively. "I guess I am." Just

saying the words was unexpectedly empowering; if I claimed to be a tramp, who was going to argue? "What about you?"

"Oh, sure."

I continued along the road, pondering that exchange. I was certainly closer to being a tramp than when I began. But as far as actually *being* one—that was stretching things. I still thought about my family, about my friends, about girls I missed at school. My professors would still accept collect calls. I had still been more nervous than a tramp should have been entering the Havre jungle.

Yet a change had occurred. In part because my own desire was so strong, the jungles were becoming my home. For weeks I had been concerned with appearances: Did I look like a tramp? When tramps looked at me, would they see themselves? Those seemed the most important things. But now I saw that I had neglected what was going on inside. Sloughing off that *feeling* of being an outsider, a stranger that did not belong, was essential to achieving the ease of mind and manners that would make tramps see me as one of them. "Yeah, I guess I am," I had said, and it struck me that, to a degree, saying it made it so.

In a book I mentioned earlier, *Tally's Corner*, Elliot Liebow made the same point, explaining how he, educated and white, had gotten to know his subjects. Through slight adjustments to his dress and way of speaking, "I had dulled some of the characteristics of my background." Parts of his appearance, speech, and general way of being were beyond his power to change, but he notes this wasn't all for the worse: "The disadvantage of being white was offset in part by the fact that, as an outsider, I was not a competitor" for the scant financial opportunities they pursued, nor for the same sorts of social status. One day early on, he wrote, he met nine men, learned the names of several more, and spent many hours on the corner. "And perhaps most important of all," he continued, "in my own mind I had partly sloughed off that feeling of being a stranger and achieved that minimum sense of 'belonging' which alone permits an ease of manner and mind so essential in building personal relationships." The section closes with this recap: "In retrospect, it seems as if the degree to which one becomes a participant is as much a matter of perceiving oneself as a participant as it is of being accepted as a participant by others."

I have left my regular life and immersed in others' often enough that I've developed some awareness of what happens during that process. I don't think of it as being incognito when I immerse, and I don't really like the phrase undercover, as it has overtones of a law enforcement investigation into illicit activity. I'm not going in to "get the goods" on my subjects, but rather in order to understand them. In the course of trying to see things their way, of being empathetic, I often begin to identify with them, to think and speak in terms of "we."

Have I left my skin for someone else's? That's not how I look at it. Rather, I think of identity as a range of possibilities; each of us, as we move through life, settles on a certain congeries of characteristics. Living a different way requires us to emphasize a *different* set of characteristics. My wife is fond of saying, for example, that my months in corrections awoke my "inner disciplinarian." In other words, that one part of me was emphasized, underscored, for the duration of the immersion. If required, I can muster qualities that I'm happy not to need in my everyday, normal life (such as saying *no* repeatedly during the day!). Not that I necessarily like it, more just that, yes, I can play that role. I can be that person. (In my mind, this is different from being an actor, and possibly more difficult. An actor can go back to "being himself" right after a performance, but an immersion writer may inhabit another world, and a somewhat different persona, for days, weeks, or months.)

Of course, it is entirely possible to do extensive participatory fieldwork in a way that does not mess as much with one's sense of self. I have done that, too. If one is retaining more of an identity as an observer (I've always liked that phrase from the United Nations, "permanent observer status"), then one might feel less a sense of empathy or oneness. Getting what you need, if you do not connect on a deep level with your subjects (which might be a perfectly reasonable response, depending on what they're like), may simply depend on your capacity for forbearance, and toleration. In other words, how well can you put up with being around those not quite like you or your friends? How much "otherness" can you stand?

Ethics

Questions of ethics are at the heart of much journalism. In the old days people debated whether journalism was *objective*; whatever was not deemed objective was *slanted*, and when I started writing, slanted meant bad. These days, though, perhaps in recognition that all media have a bias of some sort and that true objectivity is elusive or impossible, people speak more productively of whether a piece of writing is *fair*. Conversations about fairness tend to address the question of interest: whose interest does this article/book/film serve? Is it balanced or one-sided? Empathetic or narcissistic? A candid exploration or a doctrinaire assertion?

When it comes to immersive writing, or really any long-form project where the author didn't simply interview people but spent time in their world over an extended period, a special set of ethical questions can arise upon publication.‡ People will ask themselves, as they read, *did this writer treat the subject(s) fairly?*

Readers often appreciate, in other words, that a writer has some power over her subject. The writer gets to decide what to include, what to leave out—how to cast the story. Simply put, the writer gets to tell the story in her own words.

Where it gets tricky is that, even in the most deferential case—a writer trying to "channel" or champion the subject—the writer's take is likely to vary in certain ways from the subject's. The writer has worked hard to create a fair portrait, and probably done a better job of making the story accessible to the public than the subject could—that's why she's a writer, after all. But then the subject reads it and is unhappy.

Sometimes the subjects of our articles are unhappy over very small things, things the writer might never have predicted would be a problem. Maybe the writer described the subject's dog as "well-fed," and the pet's roundness turns out to be a sore spot with the subject. I once got a massage from an American masseuse at a resort I was writing about in Fiji, and quoted her as saying that Fiji had no indigenous massage tradition. That prompted an indignant letter to the editor, informing me I was mistaken. That sort of thing can happen with all kinds of writing.

Sometimes the issues are a little bigger. A writer I'm friends with had an assignment to profile a teenage athlete. He spent a lot of time with him, but called me, upset, four or five months into the project. The young man, he said, starting to feel more com-

---

‡ If the writing was for a class or otherwise remains unpublished, then these ethical concerns are much less urgent: nobody but a teacher, perhaps, and others you show it to will know what the story said. I always ask my students to promise confidentiality to each other over the pieces they are working on. That takes pressure off, as students can feel free to experiment without worrying about hurting anyone's feelings.

fortable with him around, had begun to use racial epithets. What should he do? Would he be whitewashing his subject if he did not include this tendency in the piece?

First check with your editor, I told him: that person might have an opinion. But, I continued, if I were your editor, I'd probably tell you to be up-front with the guy about your personal reaction, and urge him to modulate his comments; explain that you weren't going to "out" him for this, but that it made him look like a hick and could hurt his career. Make it sound like practical advice; don't be sanctimonious about it. As for justifying not outing him, I said I didn't think my job was to police the thinking or attitudes of everybody I write about. If this person were a teacher or a mayor or community leader, these racist attitudes would be germane to my article and I would write about them. But for a profile of a young athlete, I'd be less certain. Whatever you do, I said, don't keep your true feelings a secret, because by doing that we start to dig ourselves a hole.

Where immersion writers find their worst trouble, I believe, is over questions of honesty and betrayal, of dissembly and deception. Why would a writer deceive a subject? Mainly, I think, in order to get them to talk, to share without fear of being criticized. Subjects can be nervous; the writer wants them to open up. But deceiving our source, even when that person is not a good person, is a bad idea. The worst-case scenario of a writer deceiving a subject was the subject of Janet Malcolm's now-classic *The Journalist and the Murderer*, originally a two-part article in the *New Yorker*. Malcolm described the research behind the bestselling book *Fatal Vision*, about a Green Beret doctor, Jeffrey R. MacDonald, accused of murdering his pregnant wife and two daughters in 1970. MacDonald believed that the author, Joe McGinniss, was firmly on his side; at trial, he even allowed the writer to sit at the table with his legal team. McGinniss professed solidarity with the accused at every step.

During the trial, though, McGinniss claimed later, he became convinced of MacDonald's guilt. He proceeded to write a book that depicts MacDonald as a stone-cold psychopath. MacDonald, in prison, had no idea what McGinniss had done until he agreed to be interviewed about the book by the television show, "60 Minutes." With the cameras rolling, correspondent Mike Wallace read aloud to MacDonald from a proof copy; his reaction, in Malcolm's words, was one of "shock and utter discomposure."

A lawsuit ensued, and huge sales. McGinniss's reputation, I think it's fair to say, never recovered.

That's an extreme example. Most questions of betrayal in writing never come close to that epic scale. More commonly, subjects will tell the writer something personal that does not reflect well on them. Maybe it's an off-color joke, maybe it's a racist or anti-Semitic remark. What is the immersive writer to do? Taking exception, the writer could feel, might hurt rapport. On the other hand, isn't the writer bound to tell the truth above all else? And, in terms of literary value, aren't readers better served by a warts-and-all portrayal than one that pulls its punches?

Experience suggests to me a few ways to avoid these tough dilemmas. The first is, never pretend to agree with something that you don't agree with. At the very least, don't pretend for long. Silence is sometimes okay; the only way journalists are able to interview those with political views they disagree with is to keep their own politics off the table. Where it gets tricky is over time, in the long term: you can't just keep listening without responding (unless you are engaged in undercover reporting); if the person asks your opinion, you may need to tell him. Hedge if necessary, but don't pretend to agree. If you do, your subject may come to think you are a very different person from the person you are, and when your piece gets published, there may be an awful reckoning.

What puts immersion writers in a unique category is the long time frame. Over time, the interviewer/interviewee relationship typically becomes less formal. The two sides grow more familiar with each other, and it can become easy for the subject to forget that the writer is there to take notes, to observe, to notice. A subject, after a few days or weeks of acquaintance, might make an offhand remark of the sort one would make to a friend, forgetting that in fact, he is speaking to a writer. It's up to the writer to remind him. There are various ways one can do this: pull out the notebook and say, *Is that on the record?* Or repeat aloud the thing just said and then ask, *Is that something I can quote?* Not every researcher is going to want to take these steps, because it is easier just to let a person talk, and not be monitoring every conversation for things the person might later regret saying. And in fact, that place of greater candor and honesty is what most interviewers seek: we want evidence of the real person speaking, not the self who's been preparing for an interview. But it's not fair to let a person put his guard down and not remind him what's going on. And if you don't do it, and you later quote him saying something he'll regret, he may respond with anger and even deny that he said it.

It has taken many immersive experiences, and my own share of missteps, to figure this out. I haven't always done the right thing, through inattention, inexperience, or just faith that I, being a good person, was justified in having a few extra cards in my hand. But time, and years of teaching, have taught me that I'll feel better about the process, and my subjects will, if I keep them from blathering heedlessly.

My most recent experience was one of the best. I wrote about a large animal veterinarian in Iowa, for *Harper's*, visiting three times over the course of a year for about a week each time, and emailing and checking in via phone many times more. But I almost didn't make it past the first visit. Soon after I arrived at his clinic on a Monday morning, he asked me to come out back with him where we could speak alone. He basically said this: *Listen, I've got a lot at stake here. I don't know you, and if I let you tag along on all my calls, how do I know you aren't going to make me look bad? I'm proud of what I do and the choices I make, but what if you don't feel the same? Will I be able to read your article before it goes to print?*

I told him no, that the magazine wouldn't allow him to read it in advance, though they would call him up and fact-check everything I had written—so at the very least, he'd be protected against falsehoods. But I also knew that wouldn't protect him against what he was worried about. I responded, more or less, like this: *You are right to be worried, I said. You are making yourself vulnerable and another writer could treat you unfairly. But I promise I will not. I admire how you're making a go of it in a harsh economic environment; I don't begin with ill will. Because I'm a journalist I tend to be skeptical, but how about this: At the end of each day, before we part ways, I'll tell you if I saw anything that made me uneasy. I won't keep any reservations to myself. There will be no surprises. I'll listen to what you say and pay close attention. And that should let you see what's on my mind early on, while it's still easy to pull the plug. And should you decide to do that, I won't have any hard feelings.*

The vet agreed, and that, essentially, is what we did. I asked him about feeding cattle antibiotics they don't need and the pain caused by dehorning and castration. One of his methods of castration, I observed, did seem to cause the bulls a lot of pain. He explained why he did it that way. I quoted those conversations in the article; we had several of them. I also consulted veterinary experts in bovine pain, including one at the vet's alma mater. They both thought he could do things differently, but they helped me to understand why he probably did it the way he did. *Harper's* let me examine the matter in detail. And when the article was published, and the vet read that section for the first time, he was satisfied. It wasn't quite how he would have put it, he said, but he could see that I worked hard on it, and I talked to the right people. And, what you usually hope for but don't always achieve with long-form pieces: we're still friends.

Friendship

Allow me to point out that that last assertion, "we're still friends," is not true, in the usual sense of the term. That veterinarian, whom I like a lot, is not like my other friends. I won't send him a holiday card or call him on his birthday. I don't expect he'll ask to sleep on my couch the next time he visits New York City. When he invited *me* to sleep in his guest room on my visits to Iowa, I declined and stayed in a motel. I wanted to maintain some professional distance, so that if he didn't feel my article was fair, he wouldn't feel betrayed by a friend. Rather, I meant I kept him as a *professional* friend.

I employed the same restraint during my months as a correction officer. A handful of times, fellow officers invited me over to watch a game or have a beer on a day off. I always declined, even though I would have loved knowing more about their home lives: it just seemed too invasive. The secretive nature of the research made it even more so. How would I have felt, I thought, if I learned I had invited an undeclared journalist into my home, where he drank my beer, met my spouse, used my bathroom, and, let's say, held my toddler? Pretty bad—even if no part of that made it into his book.

To me this is a question of boundaries. It's just better this way, seems fairer. Maybe I miss out on collecting some wonderful detail, but ... you can't have everything. To me, the idea of becoming an *actual friend* of a subject is the same thing as moving all the way to the right on that scale of participant-observation. It's losing all distance; it's going native. It's much, much better not to go there.

I don't mean to suggest, by these two examples, that I have always struck the right balance with my relationships, and most writers I know who engage in this work worry about the right balance all the time. That's because, as difficult as it can be to gain initial access, once you have it can be surprisingly easy to become too close. The first time you experience a subject starting to treat you like a friend, you might mistake the warmth as a gift from heaven: *Now* he wants to tell me *everything!* I'm golden! But resist those overtures. It's important if you want to minimize the chance of bitter feelings down the road.

Another reason not to get too close is that, should you discover something needs to be said that will displease your subject, you need to feel free to say it. Joan Didion, in the preface to *Slouching towards Bethlehem*, famously wrote, "Writers are always selling somebody out." That's because, as far as I can tell, good writing sometimes requires it. The writer's first duty is to the integrity of the writing, not to the relationship with the source. You may not consider yourself a bad person or a mean writer, but speaking the truth may require you to burn a bridge. For your own self-preservation, as well as concern for the other person, be wary of investing too much of yourself in that relationship.

I should point out two exceptions to these scenarios. First, writers are not always the manipulators and subjects our pawns. Subjects who are media-savvy and want good publicity may try to manipulate the writer and orchestrate a certain impression. They may feign friendship to secure a favorable result. A journalist friend of mine who spent a lot of time with a Brooklyn band in the course of preparing a profile felt a real connection to them, and liked the idea that, once his article was published and the work-related phase of the relationship was over, they might become part of his circle of actual friends. But once the (favorable) profile appeared, he never heard from them again. At least he proceeded the right way, saving the cultivation of actual friendship for after publication.

The other exception is when you write about people who, due to the very nature of their situation, you are unlikely to criticize. Such as children. Alex Kotlowitz, in the epilogue to *There Are No Children Here*, reveals that in addition to paying some of their small living expenses (such as for jeans and sneakers) during his research, after it he helped both boys get into private school and helped pay their tuition. Following the book's publication, Kotlowitz became Pharaoh's de facto guardian and the boy lived with his family until his graduation from high school. I can't imagine anyone saying Kotlowitz did the wrong thing.

WHAT TO LOOK FOR
How to Take Notes

A few years ago I made a guest visit to a writing program at a large university in New England. Details about the workshop, the talk, the dinner with faculty afterward I have forgotten, but one thing about the visit remains vivid in my mind. A young man at work on a nonfiction MFA degree came up after my talk and told me about the weeks he had recently spent among American soldiers in Iraq. Sounds fascinating, I said, and asked if he was writing about the experience now. Well, he had been, he answered, but he'd had to stop. Then he confessed the reason: he hadn't taken any notes, and as a result he would have to go back. At first I didn't quite understand: *no notes at all?* I asked. He tried to explain: most of his peers were writing personal essay or memoir, and the only resource they felt they needed (or which they had been taught to value) was their memory. He had toured Iraq the same way, thinking memory would be enough. And I suppose there are cases in which it

BOX 1. THE IRB

Before I got a job teaching at a university, I had never heard of an Institutional Review Board. But academic researchers in subjects such as anthropology, sociology, political science, and psychology know them well. Most universities have an IRB, and some colleges do as well. Their charge is to oversee research done on human subjects by members of the university community (professors, researchers, and sometimes students), and make sure it is conducted ethically. IRBs were established partly in response to abusive biomedical research in the mid-twentieth century, such as the Tuskegee syphilis study (in which treatment was intentionally withheld from infected patients), experiments on prisoners by Nazi physicians that involved wounding and other tortures, and experiments involving radiation during the Cold War.

Other concerning studies were behavioral, such as the Milgram obedience experiment, the Stanford Prison Experiment, and the MKULTRA mind control studies organized by the CIA.

While IRB oversight is appropriate to much research, the stories I've heard make me think that most if not all of the research I'm describing in this book would be difficult to carry out with an IRB involved. Typically, for example, IRBs require, in advance of research, a detailed plan for which people will be contacted and what will be asked of them; they often continue their oversight during the period of research as well. Signed consent forms are routinely required from anybody interviewed. These two aspects of IRB oversight are a big problem when you're working on a book or article that is topical, and time is of the essence; the better periodicals are not going to wait weeks or months for an academic committee to render a decision on how to research a subject that might be breaking news.

Another incompatibility with journalism is an insistence in most ethnographic-type research that the human research subjects be anonymized—in other words, not named. One can see how this requirement was designed to protect people. But it takes away the incentive to participate by people who might *want* publicity (such as activists, or those in business), and further, and worse, it takes away accountability by anyone involved in a story who hasn't acted honorably. Anonymizing can also obscure fudging of data by the researcher.

As I waited to get hired by the USDA as a meat inspector, a book review editor sent me an early copy of *Every Twelve Seconds: Industrialized Slaughter and the Politics of Sight* (2011). Author Timothy Pachirat, then a doctoral candidate in political science at Yale, got hired at a beef slaughterhouse in Omaha and conducted secretive participant-observation for five and a half months. The book is fascinating: Pachirat worked alongside inspectors like the one I hoped to become, and offered a detailed, nuanced, first-person view of life inside the plant. But where was the plant exactly? He wouldn't say. What was the company called? He didn't reveal that, either. Rather, he explained, "from the start my decision to access the kill floor as an entry-level worker without informing the management of my intention of writing about my experiences has included a commitment not to directly expose a specific slaughter house or individuals." A foot-note explains that this "com-mitment" was developed in conversations with "an over-sight committee." I didn't understand it at the time, but academic friends have sug-gested to me that the commit-tee was Yale's IRB, and that their restrictions likely tied Pachirat's hands. He was prob-ably *required* to anonymize the slaughterhouse. I can see why you might protect the privacy of individuals, but why protect a corporation? How are you going to speak truth to power, as a writer, if you cannot name the powerful?

Professors and students in academic journalism pro-grams in the United States are exempted from IRB oversight. This is absolutely necessary: the best journalism cannot be practiced under the oversight of a cautious, slow-moving board. I have met determined and enterprising social scien-tists who are working to man-age and reform the IRBs at their institutions in order to produce work that is timely and relevant for an audience beyond the academy. I hope they succeed.

might be . . . but what about writing down quotes? What about writing down the names of soldiers, and where they were from? He figured he'd just be changing their names anyway, he said, as memoir writers sometimes do, so why distract himself/interrupt his experience/divert his attention with note-taking?

I didn't need to convince him that was a bad idea; he'd already concluded it, belatedly. But I should probably articulate my think-ing here so that you don't make a similar mistake. If you are seek-ing out an experience that you intend to write about, taking notes should be a major part of it. Maybe, if you're a committed personal essayist, it will just be a journal you update over coffee, or before bed. Or, if you're a literary journalist, it can be lines scribbled in a small spiral notebook and/or typed into a laptop or mobile device more or less continually during the day. The point is twofold: (1) notes will only bolster your memory, not detract from it, and (2) specificity (names, quotes, ranks of officers, data like hometowns or what was eaten in a meal or tattooed on an arm or smelled at dusk) gives writing power. It also gives you the option of writing journalism, which requires the citing of actual data, not just best-I-could-remember data.

You need notes.

v v v

Taking notes is a conscious means of reflecting on what we've experienced: seen, heard, tasted, smelled. Obviously notes are a way of remembering things, but every bit as important, notes are a way of noticing.

What's important? What matters to you, and why? Taking notes requires knowing, or at least having a vague idea about, what you're interested in. If I were to be abducted by space aliens I suppose that practically everything I experienced would be interesting, at least in the beginning. But when spending time with mere mortals, one needs to think about a subset of "practically everything," because "everything" is overwhelming. If you tend to know intuitively what's interesting, you can skip the next several paragraphs. But if you're sometimes unsure, then stick with me.

One set of questions about an impending personal experience, and/or people we're studying, can come from our friends. Oh, said mine at college, you're heading out to hop freight trains? We'd like to know about

- how you physically hop a train
- what's most dangerous about it (is it the police? the risk of falling off?)
- if it's scary
- how you get the hoboes to talk to you
- whether they still leave those secret symbols on fences, gates, etc., that tell other hoboes which farmers are friendly, which have mean dogs, etc.

In writing for a general audience, it behooves you to answer the things everyone wants to know.

Themes and Meanings

But you'll also want to go beyond those obvious, first-level questions and look for a set of deeper understandings. In other words, once you've hopped some trains, figured out the police, spoken with hoboes, learned that the secret language is a thing of the past, and calmed your palpitating heart, a whole new world of insider information will open up for you. It will contain ideas about the life and what it means. Some may be obvious; others will be harder to grasp.

How is their life different from mine? I recall asking myself. How is it different from a middle-class person's? And how is it different from an urban homeless person's? Do hoboes have a different set of values than most people? Have they purposely sought out a space on the edge of society, or have they been pushed there? Is the "romance of the rails"—the freedom of going where you want, when you want, with whomever you want, and preferably in a westerly direction—something hoboes feel, or is it mainly the fantasy of people on the outside? These questions led me to pursue a particular theme in my research: is this life freedom, or is it poverty?

But I didn't work that theme out until I was well along. One thing that helped me was that book my anthropology professor gave me on the eve of my journey. *Participant Observation*, by James Spradley, introduced me to a number of ethnographic concepts and overall seemed a helpful guide for what I hoped to do. Parts of it were arcane and unnecessarily complicated, but others suggested a path for pursuing meaning and focus in "the field."

The gist of the ethnographic approach, the book made clear, is to look for meaning from *inside* a culture. Spradley urges the investigator to seek out "cultural themes," sometimes implicit but other times articulated explicitly in phrases or slogans. I realized I was hearing one of these the second or third time I listened to my companions, who preferred to be called tramps, explain to me the difference between a tramp, a hobo, and a bum. As the tramp I call Lonny explained, it was a hierarchy, with the tramp on top:

"Well, you see, the tramp travels, and he works. You work sometimes, dontcha?" I nodded. "Well then, that's like us. Now the hobo, he travels, but he don't work. Just likes driftin'. The bum ain't gonna do nothin', work or travel—that bum don't do shit!"

In other words, tramps explicitly valued travel and the work ethic. They would criticize others as lazy—an observation at odds with a popular view, expressed in old songs like "Hallelujah, I'm a Bum" and "Big Rock Candy Mountain," that these itinerants were proud of not working. A bit later in the chapter, Spradley lists cultural arenas in which themes might be found:

- social conflict
- cultural contradictions
- informal techniques of social control

Each of these had meaning in the world I was becoming a part of. For social conflict, it was tramps running up against railroad and town police, and also against local homeless people (whom they called "home guard," after the men who stayed home instead of joining the military during World War II). For cultural contradictions, in which a group of people say one thing but do another, it was the idea that tramps actually work. From my perspective, most of these self-professed tramps were, according to their own definition, hoboes. (Even more ironic, the travelers they assigned to the bottom-most rung of the status ladder, Mexican migrants, seemed to very much fit the proud definition of tramp, clearly traveling in order to find jobs.) And for informal techniques of social control, I noticed that a force for social coherence, in their Hobbesian world of every man for himself, was the idea of "running partners" or "partnering up." Once you partnered with somebody, they no longer heedlessly ate and drank whatever they wanted; they had to *share*. ("It's like the musketeers," a hobo named Pistol Pete explained to me. "All for one and one for all.")

More broadly, Spradley attended to concepts like time and space—and the different ways members of different subcultures experienced both of them. Hobo time, based on the uncertainty of train schedules, the desire to be in a warmer part of the country when the season turned cold, and the need to conform to the opening hours of a food stamp office or rescue mission, was very different from the time experience of "squares" who followed a 40-hour work week. Often there was too much time, and boredom; one solution to boredom was drinking, which, I realized while drinking with them, made boredom go away. Alcohol eases the passage of time. Hoboes' experience of American space, both within towns and between towns, differed from other Americans', as well. All of this suggested things I might want to look for, take notes on, and ultimately write about.

So what do you take notes about? Anything that's interesting, of course, but *definitely* about the ideas that are swirling around in your mind. Your goal will be to bring this social world to life, through incident and anecdote and some trenchant lines, here and there, about what all of this *means*. Taking notes makes you think; along the way or at the end, insights may spring from them.

Reporting for Story

A summer spent with Polynesian pearl divers could appeal to an economist interested in the gem market, an environmental scientist interested in degradation of the oceans, a newspaper feature writer, or an immersion journalist. All of these researchers will take notes, for notes constitute the raw material out of which we fashion finished writing. But the notes of the immersion journalist are going to be different from the notes of the other researchers. One of the ways they'll be different is that the immersion writer, generally speaking, will be preparing to write a narrative—to literally tell a story.

In other words, she is not planning to address a small audience of experts who use a highly specialized vocabulary, and she's probably not mustering the data critical for a narrow analysis or argument. She's interested in writing down what the divers and others actually say, but not simply in order to "get quotes"—she wants her readers to know what they sound like, how they talk. Speech and dialogue are two of the building blocks needed for writing narrative. Here are some others:

- Characters. Do you have any? Do they make a one-time appearance, or do you follow them all the way through?

- Scenes. Is there action that happens in a place, where you could "set a scene"? Is there enough happening that you could accrue a collection of scenes? (One of the most basic kinds of narrative is simply a succession of linked scenes.)
- Chronology and change. Does the story develop through time? Do the characters undergo transformation? Are there meaningful incidents? Is there any chance you might have rising action and resolution—a narrative arc?
- Back story. Are there relevant events that preceded your arrival? Pay attention to them: you don't need to have witnessed events in order to recount them if you're well-informed.
- Trouble. Trouble is interesting. Unlike in real life, where you might choose to avoid trouble, in researching a story you must attend to it. Trouble is news; trouble is a way to advance a story.
- First-person narrator. Is the person telling the story an "I?" Does this "I" interact enough with others and reveal enough about themselves that they, too, become a character? (As mentioned previously, first-person narration is not required. Nor is, strictly speaking, a narrative arc. These and other matters will be revisited in chapter V.)

It's harder to write narrative after the fact if you weren't thinking of it all along. On the other hand, you don't want to go overboard and come to your research with a story predetermined: you need to be open to surprise. What I call reporting for story begins with simply an awareness of what you might need. Essentially, it means paying extra attention in your research to elements of narrative. Instead of spreading your attention across the entire volleyball squad, perhaps you'll choose to develop characters by focusing on a subject—say, on the coach, the captain, the libero, and . . .

a player who is struggling (because remember, trouble is interesting). Are there rivalries? Are there antagonists and peacemakers? Who are they? Whose presence/story can help explain the team's interpersonal dynamics?[§]

What are some possible scenes? A handful of high-stakes games (games against rivals, games for a championship, games where a player is back after an injury) might provide some. But also, perhaps, what's happening in the locker room or on the bus ride home after a defeat. The coach taking a girl aside for a talking-to. Or the coach and the captain brainstorming strategy for the next game. Remember that many scenes will be helped if you have quotes—a record of what was actually said, either in conversation between two or more people (a voice recorder helps here) or by an individual in response to your questions.

What is truly interesting and should be examined in detail, and what is less interesting and might be compressed (or ultimately ignored)? *There is no necessary correspondence, in a writing project, between the amount of time you spend paying attention to a particular person or event, and the number of words you'll spend describing them in your piece.* Now and then, a writer needs to stand back and take the measure of the whole. Just because a passage is well written doesn't mean you need to keep it. As a famous novelist once said, a necessary power in a writer is the ability to *kill your darlings*—to discount something that once seemed precious but, in retrospect or when taking the broad view, is less so.

Also, good writers often vary the focal length of their attention. Some things need to be observed close up—the skinned knee, the bruise, the rip in the jersey, or the hand on the shoulder. Other things might best be observed from a distance—not from

---

[§] For examples of how one writer successfully chose characters in this situation, see Madeleine Blais, *In These Girls, Hope Is a Muscle.*

the coach's bench, in other words (though your access to that bench is precious), but maybe from that one bleacher toward the back where the same old-timer who is the team's No. 1 fan always sits, week after week. What does he see from back there—what changes from season to season, year to year? Think of switching from a close-up, perched-on-the-shoulder view to what might be called "God view" (the most encompassing perspective possible), and back again. Take notes about each.

And remember to always think. Taking notes doesn't mean simply "soaking it all up." It means paying attention. To paraphrase Henry James, you want to be the person on whom nothing is lost. You want to notice things, like this: I once attended an early spring meeting in my neighborhood of people interested in beekeeping. The woman leading the meeting was dressed in black but arrived wearing a yellow parka. In other words, she was dressed in the colors of a bee! As the meeting broke up I asked her if that was intentional, dressing in black and yellow. "What do you mean, intentional?" she asked. She totally didn't get it; she didn't know what I was talking about. But to me, her way of dress was a telling detail—in other words, a simple observation that connotes a larger meaning. If I were to write about that meeting, I might look for a way to include that.

Active and Passive Research

And speaking of perspective, reporting for story to me means being creative in gaining the perspectives you need. "Hanging out" or being "a fly on the wall" is a great strategy, as long as what's happening in the room is worth your while. But if you're bored there, then maybe it's time to fly to another room.

As an example: I mentioned that my research at Sing Sing prison continued longer than I might have preferred just because

I didn't know enough, hadn't seen enough. Vividly I remember my literary agent (who is also a brilliant coach and editor) asking me at several points along the way, *Who are your main characters? What happens to them? What happens to you? How and when does the story end?* I considered that last question to be easy: "It ends the day I quit," I said, somewhat stupidly. She gave me a look, and asked about Christmas, New Year's, the end of the year. I told her I'd heard that New Year's Eve was supposed to be particularly crazy in B Block, the building I was most familiar with, which had a large number of young prisoners, more recent arrivals. "They say at midnight they set fires," I explained. Her eyes widened and she gave me the same kind of look a therapist might, when you've just said something that answers your own question. "What? Work that night? It's not my shift—I'm mornings," I replied. Again the stare. I didn't play dumb. "Okay, I see. Yes, maybe I could swap shifts with somebody." It turns out I did (it was easy—nobody wants to work on New Year's Eve), and in that night I discovered the ending to *Newjack*—the title of that last chapter is "The Fires of the New Year." I didn't change the action by playing director—by telling the prisoners to light the fires, or distributing matches. Rather, I got myself into a position where I could see the action.

Sometimes, it is only through collaboration with your subject that you will be able to witness, or take part in, a particular scene. I wrote a long profile of Ophelia Dahl, a founder (with Paul Farmer and Jim Yong Kim) of the groundbreaking NGO called Partners in Health. Dahl, who is somewhat publicity-averse, hoped that a day spent with me at her offices in Boston would provide the material I needed. I knew, though, that being able to accompany her to Haiti, where the organization famously began, would give me better scenes and add a lot of interest. It took persistence on my part, but she finally agreed and helped me set it up. We sat together on the plane and on various harrowing drives, all of it potential material.

In a similar vein, for my book *The Routes of Man* I got permission to live with Israeli soldiers for a time, and to watch as they staffed the highway checkpoints that control Palestinian movement in the West Bank. My next goal was to accompany Palestinians as they negotiated some of these same checkpoints. A Palestinian waiter named Sameh dropped by my hotel in Nablus one evening for what he thought would be a one-time interview. Yes, he confirmed, he worked at a restaurant in Jerusalem; in fact, he'd be returning there in the morning. Later he added that the trip would be difficult, because he worked in Jerusalem without Israeli permission. My heart pounding, I saved my request till the end of the interview, after he'd gotten to know me better. *Could I come with you tomorrow?* I asked. Sameh had to think about it a few minutes, but finally he said yes. He gave me directions to his mother's house, from which we'd leave at 8 AM. I half-expected to arrive there and find him already gone, or have him tell me he had changed his mind.

Instead I sat by his side as we hired taxis that evaded checkpoints, as we walked a long loop around another checkpoint, and as soldiers at a checkpoint that he thought would give him no trouble made him wait for about two hours. Finally we hid behind a wall in West Jerusalem (the Israeli side) and jumped out to hail a cab for East Jerusalem (the Palestinian side, where Sameh shared an apartment). When we walked into the lobby of his apartment building late in the day, Sameh smiled and said, "So now you have seen it. My home in Jerusalem." He reached out to shake my hand goodbye.

But I had been expecting to see the room in which he actually lived, and told him so. He blanched a bit, consulted some other young men in the lobby, and finally took me there, up several flights of dark stairs to his room. The building, he eventually explained, was not approved for habitation—it had no water, and he was there illegally. I thanked him for showing it to me, promised not to reveal its exact location, and knew I had gotten a good scene for my book.

In sum: a limitation of nonfiction narrative, in contrast to fiction, is that the writer is largely unable to control the events he'll describe. He can't make it up. That said, nonfiction research offers manifold opportunities to be creative. Along with observing (and taking notes on) the various things unfolding around him, he must periodically ask himself: What can I get for a scene? Who that I've met is a likely character? What could I do with them, where could I go, that offers the potential for something interesting to observe? Where is the action and how can I get there? With experience you get better at *steering your research*. Remember, research is a creative act.

A Note on Media

Everybody devises his or her own best way to take notes; I am not going to prescribe one. That said, I can give some advice.

At a minimum everybody needs a way to jot down thoughts quickly: a name, a title, a word in another language, a joke, a question. Some sort of small paper notebook, kept in a handbag or pocket or knapsack, near a writing instrument or two, is the common solution. It can be a fancy Moleskine or the cheapest spiral-bound jotting pad from a dollar store. Because convenient size and expansive canvas for great thoughts don't often go together, most people pair a small paper notebook with a larger theme notebook or a computer, often a laptop, but increasingly a tablet (sometimes with a keyboard). The larger thing is useful when one is comfortably situated with a bit of time, the smaller thing when one is on the go.

Personally, I love typed-out notes. They are easy to read, easy to augment (if you remember something later), easy to search, and easy to back up. My personal workflow usually involves taking notes on-the-go with a pen and a notebook small enough to fit in my back pocket, and then rewriting and expanding on those notes at the end of the day or week on my computer. When I go too long without transcribing and rewriting on a computer, I get nervous. After three weeks of fascinating travel with a convoy of Kenyan truck drivers from Mombasa, without anything to type on, I was relieved to get to war-torn Rwanda because I could make a copy of my notes and mail it home. It cost me nearly $100 to do so, but the feeling was akin to, say, locking in gains by selling shares in a penny stock that has appreciated astronomically (not that I actually know that feeling!).

Which reminds me that the absolutely most important thing about notes is that you never lose them. I have been haunted, for years, by something I read in the ethnography by Edmund Leach, *Political Systems of Highland Burma* (1954): having completed a part of his doctoral dissertation, he lost it, and all of his notes and photos, when the Japanese Army invaded Burma. My response to this nightmare has been to always make copies.

Ideally your notes will also consist of photographs, audio recordings, and even video. (Some of your audio and video you may choose to transcribe; other files will be valuable just in the way they refresh your memory of a scene, a voice, a feeling.) The advent of smart phones has made it much, much easier to take notes in all three media. The risk involved in *depending* on a smart phone, however, is that it will run out of power or break, when you are far from a plug or repair shop. So always remember to bring some paper and a pen along, as well.

How Deep

So you got to let me know
Should I stay or should I go?

THE CLASH

With experience, you get better at using research to consciously lay the foundation for the writing that is to follow. First I need to learn about this; I need to try that. If you plan to write narrative, you need to have thought about the story: where it begins and (as my agent stressed) where and how it ends, and what happens in between. How long you stay depends on many things, including what it is you plan to write. Some ideas seem to want to be articles, others want to be books.

For example, soon after I was hired as a correction officer by the State of New York, my default goal became an article for the *New Yorker* about my passage through the corrections academy in Albany. I thought this seven-week boot camp, the place where the profession's values are first instilled, would let me approach close-up an essential question about corrections officers: Do they arrive at the job just like anybody else and change? Or does the work attract a certain kind of person? A long article seemed the right length for that.

But on the final Friday of the academy, when my classmates and I received our job posting and I learned I'd been assigned to Sing Sing, I was glad: by that point I wanted to put my training to work, and see what a CO's job was really like. Sing Sing wasn't far from my home in the Bronx, so I knew I'd be able to continue this research, unlike if I'd been assigned to say, Attica, which was about six hours away. Beyond that, real work in a prison might let me go deep enough to write more than just an article. In my head I started planning for a book.

Another example is from my friend Matthew Power. At the time of his tragic death (in 2014, while researching an article in

Uganda), Matt was one of the most prolific and successful magazine writers I knew. He traveled the world for national magazines and got to write about everything from the human side of Manila's biggest garbage dump to the ravages of the Taliban in Afghanistan to malaria control in Cambodia and needle exchange in Vancouver, BC. I met Matt before these successes, when he enrolled in my nonfiction workshop at the Bread Loaf Writers' Conference in Vermont. But even then he seemed overqualified; the manuscript he had brought for workshopping, he confessed, had just been accepted for publication in the *Believer*. One thing he hoped to get out of the workshop, he said, was a better sense of what makes an article versus what makes a book, and the role research plays in that.

It's a difficult question. The largest part of the answer is probably this: How meaty is the topic, and what's its shelf life? Will it still be relevant in five or ten years? On a practical level, how many words will it take you to do the subject justice? (Long-form articles, as I write this, tend to run 3,000–9,000 words. General nonfiction books are commonly 90,000–120,000 words.) Lastly, how interested are readers likely to be in a long treatment of this subject? And how interested are you in devoting the time required by a book?

Two summers later I was back at Bread Loaf and received a phone call from Matt. He was at a pay phone, taking a moment's break from an expedition he was following: a group of punk anarchists had hammered together a homemade raft near Minneapolis and were floating down the Mississippi, their goal the Gulf of Mexico. He was part of the crew.

"Wow," I said. "Sounds like a book."

Well, maybe, replied Matt. But there were problems. After two weeks of floating, and growing dissension among the crew, they were still in Minnesota—floating about seven miles a day with

1,600 miles to go, as he'd later write. The captain was an ego-
maniacal Captain Ahab and Matt didn't know how long he'd be
able to endure.

I totally get it, I said. You're only human. But if you *could* endure . . .

As I learned later, Matt waited as long as humanly possible and
then walked away. The article that resulted from it, an 8,750-word
Harper's folio called "Mississippi Drift," is a small masterpiece, my
favorite of the substantial body of writing Matt left behind. Could
it have been a book? Yes, but no.

My Sing Sing and Matthew Power examples both suggest a
fairly exact correspondence between that which is researched and
that which is written about. But things could easily have worked
out differently. After a week or a month of working at Sing Sing,
I could have been discovered and fired, or not have been able to
take it, or needed at home by my wife and toddler son and infant
daughter. I might then have chosen just to write about boot camp
at the academy, even though I knew more. Similarly, Matt might
have stayed with his expedition another three weeks and made
it to Dubuque, Iowa. That wouldn't mean his narrative had to go
that long. Research produces troves of raw material, usually too
much of it. Making the transition from research to finished writing requires careful curation: things must be left out. My typed-up
daily notes for *Newjack* are about 50% longer than *Newjack* itself. A
beautiful hedge requires pruning. My friend Jay writes mostly fiction, but he uses a similar metaphor to describe moving from an
early draft (in which he includes lots of things he's unsure about)
to a more finished draft: to him it's like sculpting a big lump of
clay. The clay is your raw information, raw ideas, raw story; the finished piece is the finely-detailed figure you chisel and pinch and
inscribe, with art your goal. (Jay says he commonly throws out
50% of the clay.)

Spending time is indispensable in immersion writing. It establishes authority and knowledge. With time, otherness melts away; empathy grows. Adrian Nicole LeBlanc spent more than ten years researching *Random Family*. One hesitates to calculate her income-per-hour from this activity; it was probably pennies. This is not a choice everyone can afford to make. I do not think the book made Adrian wealthy. On the other hand, *Random Family* is enormously admired, and it will last.

Sometimes you can't wait to be done with a project. Or you have a deadline, imposed by a course, a publication, or yourself. Other times you linger. I moved to Aspen in the late 1980s with the idea of staying for a year to research a book about the town. Then I had trouble leaving—I ended up staying almost two years, I was enjoying myself so much. My book *Whiteout* includes a phrase an Aspen friend of mine used to describe that feeling: "a fright about leaving."

Sometimes you can't quite decide. Though at Sing Sing I often felt "a fright about staying" and found myself thinking how pleasant life would be once I quit, I also developed a perverse pride in my skills and ability as a correction officer, as they increased ever-so-slowly over time. I remember the night when, over dinner, I told my wife I had signed up to take the sergeant's exam. She looked at me with alarm; she too had been looking forward to a time when I wouldn't have to work on weekends, when we could tell all our friends what I had been doing, when I didn't arrive home crabby, etc. "Why would you do that?" she asked.

"Well, they only offer it every five years," I explained. "It's a lot better money."

"What are you talking about? How long do you plan to keep this job?"

"I don't know . . . just a little while longer. I mean, I doubt I'll ever actually take the exam, it's months away. But you never know."

She stared at me incredulously. "Okay," I admitted. "I'm probably not going to do it." Still she stared. "Never mind," I finally said, "I won't."

I tell this story just to illustrate how sometimes, in a long, immersive project, one of the most difficult challenges is keeping perspective. And there are no firm rules: you don't want to quit too soon. But, unless you unexpectedly discovered your calling along the way, you probably don't want to take the sergeant's exam (i.e., go native).

My best suggestion, once you've gotten your feet on the ground, is to periodically pause, step back psychically, and try to see where you are in the process. Be a writer for a weekend (or longer, if possible) and ask a writer's questions. If your goal is a book, what are the chapters? Can you outline it? Could you answer somebody like my agent, asking where the story begins, where it ends, and what happens along the way? If it's not a book, do you have enough for an article? If you have friends / advisors / editors whose opinions about this matter, consult them periodically; listen to yourself explaining to them, and listen to their answers.

IV. UNDERCOVER
MOVING BEYOND STUNT

"Man is not what he thinks he is, he is what he hides."

ANDRÉ MALRAUX, *Les Noyers de l'Altenburg*

Undercover reporting I consider the nuclear arrow in the writer's quiver, the choice when being forthright will limit the information available to you, and the topic is important enough to justify the many risks that accompany deception. Undercover research, as I wrote, can lead to hurt feelings on the part of subjects, typically places the researcher in a position of emotional and spiritual duress, as well, and can undermine the credibility of the writer.

That said, the appeal of undercover research seems obvious. Secrecy is exciting; surreptitious research promises illumination, and often delivers. Law enforcement personnel, spies, and reporters go undercover in movies and on TV in order to expose skullduggery. In so doing, they often seem to have been given a chance to reinvent themselves, to write themselves a new biography. Who wouldn't want to go undercover?

Some writers getting started in journalism are tempted to "go undercover" as a first resort, not a last. The attraction is pretty clear: it saves you the trouble of having to explain yourself and negotiate access honestly, without deception. In fiction, invisibility is often tantamount to going undercover: Harry Potter in his invisibility cloak or, going back a few years, the lead character of my former neighbor Harry Saint's novel, *Memoirs of an Invisible Man*, about a guy left invisible by a radiation accident who has a pretty good adventure seeing people without being seen.

But the drawbacks are legion. Once, at age 18, I tried to pass as Australian. My American friend Ross and I had been riding our bicycles across North America when we met Robin Weston, a charismatic Australian whose goal was to circumnavigate the globe by bicycle. After several days of riding together, our routes diverged; that night Ross and I were invited to dinner by an elderly Canadian couple in a campground. I decided to "be" Rob Weston for a night—his story was going to be mine. I adopted even his accent (so far as I could muster it), and somehow convinced them, through dessert, that I was a former vineyard worker from Coonawarra, South Australia.

Then two things happened. First of all, I was exhausted: channeling Rob Weston was a huge amount of work. The Canadians hardly asked Ross any questions at all; as an Australian, I was the exotic at the table, and they wanted to know all about me. I not only had to make up the answers to questions I didn't know the real answer to, but also had to remember those answers and make sure everything added up. Speaking in a different accent for so long was taxing, too.

But the hardest thing was living with myself once the dinner was finally over. My impersonation of Rob Weston was, in aggregate, the biggest lie I'd ever told. And for what? I had deceived the hospitable couple for no reason other than to see if I could— for my own amusement, apparently. I was ashamed of myself and waved them only the most cursory goodbye in the morning. I remember pedaling from that campground as a huge relief. What if the kindly old couple who had invited us to dinner at the campground realized I was only pretending to be an Australian? Would they have felt hurt, or angry?

Some time later, I read a page one story in the Wall Street Journal that was a precursor to today's stories about misrepresenting yourself in online dating. The reporter's first-person account described his blind dates with several women whom he met through a new innovation, the video dating service. He had not told them that he was a reporter, planning to write about it; he actually liked one of them and dated her at least three times over two months, apparently never telling her his ulterior motive. How would you feel if you were that woman, I thought? Even if he changed her name to protect her privacy, what if she read it and recognized herself—wouldn't she rightly feel used? And for no greater purpose, really, than a light feature story? (The headline and subhead, from that bygone day and age: "Look Out, Redford: Our Man Is Bursting Onto Singles Scene. He Tries 'Videodate' Singles Service And Finds It an Ego Trip.")

In a way, undercover reporting is the easy way out: a lot of the awkwardness of live research can be avoided if you simply pretend you're not doing it. But most good reporting is based upon relationships involving candor. There is no candor if your subject doesn't know what you're up to. Truthful self-representation should be the default choice for journalists and others.

Most large media have an explicit set of rules around undercover reporting, and some outright forbid it. The *New York Times*' 57-page code of ethics states: "Staff members should disclose their identity to people they cover (whether face to face or otherwise), though they need not always announce their status as journalists when seeking information normally available to the public." From what I can tell this rule exists because undercover reporting is not subject to the usual checks and balances that govern traditional journalism: sources can't always be double-checked, notes can't always be taken. It can provide cover for a journalist who is not telling the truth. A slam against undercover reporting is, "He deceived his sources. How do we know he's not deceiving us?" In the old media landscape, when there was a smaller number of big companies, part of this was protecting the brand: one lying reporter could taint the whole enterprise (as indeed has happened now and then).

Many aspiring writers reading this book, however, will not be affiliated with a major news organization (or major publisher), and will work in an environment without an explicit set of checks and balances. Therefore, it seems reasonable for the immersive writer to ask: What's okay when going undercover? And what's not?

One challenge, right up front, is to define undercover. My colleague Brooke Kroeger at New York University makes an argument at the beginning of her book, *Undercover Reporting: The Truth About Deception*, that the *Washington Post*, which forbids reporters from misrepresenting themselves, in essence allowed it in the case of a long report about substandard care at the nation's Veterans Administrations hospitals. The reporters, Dana Priest and Anne Hull (along with photographer Michel duCille), won the Pulitzer Prize for Public Service in 2008, after which details of their modus operandi became clearer: on many occasions, they had walked into the Walter Reed Army Medical Center just like patients, patients' family members, and staff would do. They did not identify themselves as reporters and evidently did not brandish notebooks, voice recorders, etc., in a way that would lend that impression. Posing as nurses or doctors would be crossing a line that the *Post* prohibits, but Kroeger asks "whether there is really a difference for a journalist between not ever telling a lie—emphasis on the word *telling*, because lies, to qualify as lies, are verbalized—and the deliberate projection of a false impression with the clear intention to mislead, to deceive?"

I tend to think there is a difference. Letting people draw their own conclusions (and not correcting misimpressions, as Priest and Hull apparently did not) is a milder form of deception than actively impersonating someone else. That said, these lines can be difficult to draw; the gray area is vast. For example, in Aspen, Colorado, I worked as a newspaper reporter (at the *Aspen Times*) and I drove a taxi (for Mellow Yellow Taxi) as ways to research my book *Whiteout: Lost in Aspen*. Most of the people I worked with at the *Times*, including the publisher and the entire editorial staff, knew I was at work on a book. I discussed it with them openly (and I had given an open-to-the-public lecture about my project early on, in town). But many of the people I spoke with in the course of reporting stories for the *Times* didn't know. Most of the other taxi drivers did not know (several worried that I was a narc), and passengers knew only when I told them. So was I "undercover" in Aspen? I never thought of it that way, and in truth, I much prefer to call my research immersive, "undercover" suggesting that the writer is trying to gain access to a conspiracy, and get the goods on people involved in wrongdoing of some kind.

But I can see why, when I am involved for weeks or months with people who do not know my real agenda, the "undercover" label might stick. It certainly has with two projects I'm proud of, my book *Newjack* and my long article for *Harper's*, "The Way of All Flesh: Undercover in an Industrial Slaughterhouse."

My employment as a New York State correction officer (CO) was preceded by an extended attempt to research their lives in a more conventional way. The *New Yorker* assigned me to write about an extended family of officers in a small community upstate. (There are many such families.) But then I discovered that the state's Department of Correctional Services wouldn't let me go to work with them; more specifically, they would allow me to have a one-time official tour of the prisons where my subjects worked, but, claiming it was too dangerous, they refused to let me visit a second time or actually see my chosen officers doing their job.

The more I thought about this refusal, the unhappier I got. Corrections was the state's No. 2 employer, after the Verizon corporation; state corrections' annual budget at the time was $1.6 billion. Yet coverage of corrections in the press was virtually nil, because administrators had decreed that their facilities were off-limits. That seemed wrong to me: this wasn't the CIA, after all. National security wasn't at stake. It was lockup, the can, the slammer— and I and every other state taxpayer paid for it. I found it difficult to believe that my safety would really be in question if I were to visit a medium-security prison, such as the first one I asked about. But the biggest reason I felt entitled to visit was that prisons were clearly a problem: record numbers of people were in them, largely a consequence of the War on Drugs and mandatory guidelines that robbed judges of discretion in sentencing. And it wasn't just anybody who got locked up; the prison population was disproportionately young men of color. There were profound issues of race, class, and punishment to consider. I felt we should be able to look inside.

So I applied to become a CO, which took far longer than I expected. I took the next civil service exam, having waited several months, and then waited a couple of years to get called for my interviews. When I filled out the job application, I hadn't lied . . . but nor did I offer any information that I didn't have to. The application didn't ask if I had written books. It's true that I had a bachelor's degree from a four-year college, but that turned out not to be so unusual. I listed my occupation as "freelance writer and researcher," which was accurate. I listed the variety of other jobs I'd held in the past—many of them on the menial side (apartment manager, SAT tutor, aerobics instructor [!]), things I had done in the early years to support my writing. Unfortunately I could not omit one that I thought could be a real red flag: reporter at the *Aspen Times*. But nobody raised an eyebrow. The only time that a question arose about my past was during a one-on-one interview with a psychologist, who had reviewed my results on a personality test. She noticed that I had spent a year in Texas as a volunteer with VISTA, the federal antipoverty program, and asked me about it. "Isn't that a little unusual," she asked carefully, "going from VISTA to corrections?" I fixed her with my best Clint Eastwood stare. "People change," I said quietly. "Okay!" she answered.

The fact that I didn't lie, and had made a photocopy of my application, turned out to be important when Random House hired an outside attorney to vet my book (see Box 3: Legal Trouble on page 120). We met later and he said it had made him feel the publisher would be in a strong position in the unlikely event they were to be sued.

I remembered that lesson some years later when I applied to become a meat inspector for the United States Department of Agriculture. I provided the name on my birth certificate where the application asked for it, as well as nicknames I'd been known by, including Ted. But I was worried by other questions, like the ones that asked me to name my employer and my duties at work. I was by this time (as I am still) a professor of journalism at New York University, which anyone with access to Google could learn. I kept my fingers crossed that they wouldn't Google "Ted Conover," however, and apparently they did not. For my duties, I dutifully explained that at NYU, "I work in the building."

My justification for applying for this job surreptitiously was that the public has an important interest in the wholesomeness of food, and that slaughterhouses, where meat is produced, are, like prisons, places a journalist can go on a tour but which otherwise are closed to the public eye. By law, however, they cannot operate without federal inspectors present. Working as an inspector, I reasoned, would both give me ongoing access to a slaughterhouse and make me intimately familiar with the ways the government attempts to protect the food supply.

Harper's magazine has been a frequent and congenial home for articles in which the writer didn't disclose his true intentions to his subjects. A collection of such pieces, published as *Submersion Journalism*, shows the variety of creative ways that surreptitious reporting can produce entertaining and compelling journalism. Among articles in the collection are an account by a writer, Kristoffer A. Garin, who signed up for a troubling love-for-hire tour ("A Foreign Affair: On the Great Ukrainian Bride Hunt") and another, by Jake Silverstein, a writer (and as of this writing, editor of the *New York Times Magazine*) who attended a convention in Reno of the Famous Poets Society ("What Is Poetry? And Does It Pay?").

Other pieces in the collection are overtly political, such as, "Bird-Dogging the Bush Vote: Undercover with Florida's Republican Shock Troops," by Wells Tower, and "Jesus Plus Nothing: Undercover among America's Secret Theocrats," by Jeff Sharlet. One can argue about whether the public interest justified the use of deception in all of these cases; this is a hard call to make. In any case, the standout in the collection is also the most creative and outrageous, "Their Men in Washington: Undercover with D.C.'s Lobbyists for Hire," by Ken Silverstein.

A longtime political correspondent, Silverstein had written many articles about the influence of money in Washington that he felt didn't get enough attention. So he contrived something dramatic. He approached various top-drawer corporate lobbying firms and presented himself as a friend of the government of Turkmenistan, which needed some help in burnishing its reputation among lawmakers. How low would lobbyists stoop in the service of a truly execrable dictatorship? As it turned out, pretty low.

He solicited proposals from several top firms, and then, armed with a voice recorder, sat down for meetings in their offices. One by one, they showed the ways that money might buy the kind of influence that could turn around a terrible reputation. Meetings could be arranged with key members of Congress and high administration officials. A media campaign could include op-eds and slots on political talk shows. Think tanks and academics could be enlisted (i.e., paid) to produce friendly papers.

Silverstein said the article attracted more attention than his many other articles about lobbyists combined. Did Silverstein lie? Indeed he did, elaborately, and some criticized him roundly for it. Was it justified? I find it hard to get upset about the hurt feelings of those lobbyists, or the time they wasted, as they are a noxious force in American democracy. On the other hand, an argument could be made that Silverstein's ruse was the leftist equivalent of the political deceptions of conservative activist James O'Keefe.

O'Keefe, in recent years, has feigned common cause with a variety of more liberal folks and caught what appear to be their damning or incriminating statements on his hidden camera. Pretending to be a pimp seeking business advice, he filmed employees of ACORN, a nonprofit community group financed in part by the federal government, counseling him on how to evade the law. The political fallout was massive; the organization lost millions in government and private funding and then closed entirely. Another time O'Keefe taped his lunch with a National Public Radio executive who apparently believed that O'Keefe was affiliated with the Muslim Brotherhood and wanted to donate $5 million. Though the NPR rep would not accept the money, he was recorded making statements critical of Tea Party conservatives and others; his boss, the president and CEO of NPR, resigned the day after the video came out.

Undercover reporting thus lends itself to spectacle, and may be used to reveal certain truths. But that's something different from the ways serious writers have used it to deepen their understanding of other social worlds. The greater promise of undercover research, to me, lies in the chance to gain an intimate insider perspective. A situation in which subjects consider the researcher "one of them" greatly ameliorates the researcher's challenge to understand *what they're doing differently because I'm here.* In that way, it may bring the native point-of-view more quickly within reach. (That being said, it's no panacea, because the undercover researcher who feels remorse about not disclosing her true motivations may also have trouble clearly apprehending what's going on around her. The undercover posture, in this scenario, may serve to *increase* the psychic distance between researcher and subject.)

A subset of immersion books involves undercover research. In addition to *Submersion Journalism*, these include *Down and Out in Paris and London*, by George Orwell; *Black Like Me*, by John Howard Griffin; *The Undesirable Journalist*, by Gunter Wallraff; *High School*, by David Owen; *My Enemy, Myself*, by Yoram Binur; *Self-Made Man* and *Voluntary Madness*, by Norah Vincent; *Working in the Shadows*, by Gabriel Thompson; and *The American Way of Eating*, by Tracie McMillan. I'll take a closer look at three of these—the books by Griffin, Binur, and Vincent—that bring some of the many complex issues around undercover reporting into sharp relief.

John Howard Griffin's *Black Like Me* is probably the best selling and most influential immersion narrative ever. Griffin, a novelist, finished high school in France and suffered wounds during World War II before returning to his hometown of Mansfield, Texas, with his wife and two kids. The town, at the time, was beset by controversy over racial segregation in its public schools. Griffin, a religious man fascinated by the ecumenism of Thomas Merton, had an idea: he would dye his skin and tour other racial hot spots in the South to bear witness to white racism and understand black self-support. Initially he wrote this as a series of reports for *Sepia*, a magazine for African Americans that was owned by a progressive white man.

In Mississippi, Alabama, Louisiana, and Georgia, Griffin found what he was looking for. A white driver wouldn't allow him to exit the Greyhound bus to use a bathroom. Another white driver who picked him up while hitchhiking made a series of lewd sexual queries. Blacks in various towns quickly taught him how to keep a low profile and stay out of trouble. Griffin was deeply rattled by all of this, and vividly narrated his growing awareness of the pain he'd been blind to during his life as a white person.

Black Like Me is short and easy to read, and had a powerful impact on the American conversation about race from its publication in 1961, close to the dawn of the civil rights era. It has lost some currency over the years, particularly as books by writers of color have gained footing in the culture, but like millions of others I read it in high school and was greatly affected.

Yoram Binur's My Enemy, Myself is a work little known in North America that I discovered while preparing to write this book. Dubbed "a Middle Eastern Black Like Me" when it was published in 1989, My Enemy, Myself describes the efforts of Binur, an Israeli and Sephardic Jew fluent in Arabic, to "get inside the mind of a Palestinian." Over several forays in 1984, Binur took up residence in a back alley hostel for Palestinian men in Tel Aviv, worked in a catering hall that hosted Israeli weddings, bused tables in a Tel Aviv restaurant, dated an Israeli woman who thought he was an Arab, and spent time in a Gaza refugee camp. The book is upsetting in many of the same ways as Black Like Me; particularly memorable is a scene in which he is washing dishes at night in a small restaurant in Tel Aviv when the owner's sister and her boyfriend decide the room in which he is working would be a good place to have sex. Afterwards,

a sort of trembling suddenly came over me. I realized that they had not meant to put on a peep show for my enjoyment. Those two were not the least bit concerned with what I saw or felt even when they were practically fucking under my nose. For them I simply didn't exist. I was invisible, a nonentity! It's difficult to describe the feeling of extreme humiliation which I experienced. Looking back, I think it was the most degrading moment I had during my entire posing adventure.

But it's the ethical dilemmas he creates with his reporting, and how unflinchingly he confronts them, that are particularly illuminating.

Soon afterwards, explaining that carnal romance between Jewish women and Arab men is fairly common, he decides that he should try to have an affair. At a club he meets Miri. "She had completed a degree in literature and she took odd jobs for a living. In English peppered with Arabic, I told her about the Balata refugee camp, where I supposedly came from." Miri takes the bait and things progress. "The lie that was in the making left me with some doubts. It was not that I had never sought out romantic ties on the basis of motives that were less than totally pure, such as the desire to find a partner for a one-night stand. In that case, though, such a desire was presumably shared by the partner. But I had never taken advantage of a woman in a cold and calculating fashion."

In bed, talking about their pasts, Binur learns that Miri's military service entailed being present during the interrogation of Palestinian women by the Shin Bet. Hearing these stories, "I felt a little like Mata Hari must have felt when she extracted information from the statesmen whom she entertained in her bed. It was mainly a sensation of power, knowing that I was able to use intimacy of the occasion for purposes which were unknown to my partner."

But clearly also it was a sensation of shame, because after the experience Binur goes on a several-day binge of drinking at home, apparently in an effort to manage his disarray. These binges are a repeating trope in the book: "For several weeks after leaving the kibbutz, I spent most of my time back in Jerusalem, lying around in an inebriated state. I was doing a poor job of relaxing; my recent experiences kept coming back to me, disrupting my peace of mind."

His countrymen's attitudes toward Palestinians, and Israel's role in their oppression, are part of what upsets him, but another part clearly is the psychic cost of his serial deceptions. The last one recounted in the book involves his sitting down with an important Palestinian political leader in a refugee camp in Gaza. Upon later learning of the deception, the man responds, "You have done a very ugly deed. How could you drink coffee in my home and dine at my table and lie to me at the same time?"

The social boundaries that Binur aimed to transgress in his project are potent indeed. I like *My Enemy, Myself* because of its boldness, its surprises (it does not follow the usual narrative of Israeli-Palestinian strife), and the author's candor: Binur shares much that lets the reader understand his process, even the parts that don't reflect well on him.

Norah Vincent's *Self-Made Man* recounts an 18-month experiment in which the author, who is lesbian, passed as a man, mostly among men: on a bowling team, as a live-in visitor to a monastery, in a strip club, going door-to-door with a sales team, and as part of a self-therapy circle. It's a book I delayed reading for years because I was put off by the cover. The paperback shows the author in two poses: seated as herself in one image, looking smart and a bit arch, and in the other as a man, looking somber and kind of sad-sack. *I can already see where this is going*, I thought, wrongly.

In fact the book is audacious, large-hearted, and exceedingly well written. Vincent makes vivid and concrete the idea of gender as a social construct. She also, by virtue (again) of her candor, has written an account that is a good place to learn about the pitfalls of undercover immersion. Vincent says her goal was to know what it was like to be a man, what it felt like, as she says about men watching women in the strip club, "to be inside that feeling."

Vincent, who describes herself as tall and with large feet (size 11.5, per an interview on the BBC), bound her breasts and used a gum compound with whisker shavings to give her face a shadow. About blending in, she says this:

> as time went on, as I became more confident in my disguise, more buried in my character, I began to project a masculine image more naturally, and the props I had used to create that image became less and less important, until sometimes I didn't need them at all.
>
> People accept what you convey to them, if you convey it convincingly enough. Even I began to accept more willingly the image in the mirror, just as the people around me eventually did.

As a member of the subset of humanity she was studying (i.e., men), I occasionally resisted Vincent's blanket comments about those of my gender. "Every man's armor is borrowed and ten sizes too big, and beneath it he's naked and insecure and hoping you won't see," she writes. Elsewhere she refers to the "ham-handed charade men were often putting on in front of each other, all of it in a desperate effort to hide that insecurity and pain." Much of this analysis seems inspired by the ideas of a book popular at the end of the last century, *Iron John: A Book About Men*, by the poet Robert Bly, a spiritual founder of what was known as the men's movement. The gender/sex role landscape has also changed significantly since the book was written; today I think men are more various, gender roles more fluid, and society overall more sophisticated about these matters. All that said, Vincent is quicker to empathize than condemn, and won my trust with comments such as,

There's nothing like a few years in the trenches of lesbian romance to give a girl a little perspective on the supposed inborn evils of the opposite sex. As time went on, I learned that girls don't behave any better than boys under relational duress, and that centuries of subjugation haven't made women morally superior.

The reader doesn't need to wait until the end of the book to find out whether her subjects ever learned of Vincent's deception; she often lets them know along the way, and shares with us their responses. A chapter called "Love," for example, which I liked least, details her dating life during this experiment. She went out with a series of women while presenting as a man. "I decided I would out myself to anyone with whom I had more than a passing, unsuccessful, date or two—which happened with three women." Each of these vignettes made me cringe. As Vincent herself acknowledges, "I was deceiving people on a lot of levels and the responsible part of me didn't feel particularly good about it." She adds, "But I also felt the glee of pulling off a performance in the real world, which meant I was lying and that I was enjoying the lie at someone else's expense." Which I think means she ultimately felt bad about that, too, as she should have.

She renders the self-outing moment as exculpatory—finally coming clean, and ready to face the consequences. (Only one person apparently got upset. Another, interestingly, said it explained a lot, because she'd begun referring to Vincent as her "gay boyfriend": "Your hair was too groomed and your shirt was too pressed, and your shoes too nice"—so much for the world always taking the undercover operative as she presents herself to it.) But to me, even the coming clean felt dirty, as though Vincent was using her confession to create a moment of entertainment for the reader.

Way back at the beginning of the book, Vincent writes, "I can say with relative surety that in the end I paid a higher price for my circumstantial deceptions than any of my subjects did." This turns out to be a foreshadowing whose meaning does not become clear until the final immersion, at a retreat weekend of the men's self-help group, at a lodge on a lake in upstate New York. Vincent has made it clear that she likes and respects a number of men in the group; they seem people more like her than the less introspective, more working-class guys she has encountered in the strip club, at the bowling alley, and on the sales team.

"The only history I had as a man was one of deceit, and with these guys it went deeper than anything before. Their safe space was carefully carved out, and I had found my way into it through a lie." The retreat is about self-disclosure and sharing, and in a somewhat shocking scene, when the group is preparing for the spirit dance, "the pinnacle of the weekend," Vincent slowly comes undone. She asks the men to cut her. She doesn't explain it to them, but admits to the reader that she wants "expiation," wants to bleed and suffer for what she's done. The men talk her out of it.

This is effectively the end of her research. Vincent says that "nervous breakdown" is too dramatic a phrase for her dissolution. "I thought my antidepressant medication had simply stopped working," she writes.

The everyday unremarkable scenery became so heavy, so imaginationless, that I felt as if I were wearing my surroundings like a cement suit. I simply quit, or some part of me did, and then left the rest of me to work out the particulars, which in my case meant checking myself into a hospital.

She then spends several pages analyzing what went wrong, almost all of which fits under the rubric offered by this sentence: "Assuming another identity is no simple affair. . . . It takes constant vigilance and energy. A lot of energy. It's exhausting at the best of times." The bittersweet, somewhat macabre postscript is that the breakdown becomes the inspiration for a second book, *Voluntary Madness: My Year Lost and Found in the Loony Bin*, an immersive account of her passage through three residential psych facilities, where she worked to pull herself back together again. She hasn't published a nonfiction book since.

v v v

The exhaustion Norah Vincent refers to just above reminded me of the exhaustion I described, at the beginning of this chapter, after my evening—just one evening—of pretending to be Australian, at age 18. This kind of thing is not for everybody.

But the upside of this deception is the excitement of adopting a new persona, of research that can produce insight, revelation, and drama. It strikes me that the less you have to mislead people (and self-disclose), and the more you can be yourself, the easier it is to perform the *deceptive* immersion of undercover reporting. Though I worked as a rookie correction officer for *Newjack*—a terribly stressful job—in a way I think I had it easier than Norah Vincent, because I didn't have to explain myself all the time, and in fact it would have been strange if I had. The uniform I wore did a lot of the talking for me. I came to identify with COs in certain important ways, and to refer to the people I worked with as "we" because all of us, in fact, were stuck in there, having to deal with difficult people all day long. Feeling common cause with my fellow COs became something to write about. Undercover reporting, as a genre, is congenial to a first-person narrator struggling to fit into a foreign world.

That does not mean that the disruption to one's psyche will always be manageable, or worth it. Deception can make other people angry. The feelings of betrayal can run deep, depending on how your subjects knew you (or thought they did)—in what capacity and for how long. And it doesn't end with anger on the part of one's subjects. Deception can damage the deceiver—if not immediately, then eventually. Binur drank to salve the wounds he inflicted on himself and others. Vincent sought several kinds of professional psychotherapeutic help, including hospitalization. This stuff is not a joke.

The most extreme examples of personal disruption from going undercover probably come from law enforcement. Kim Wozencraft's novel *Rush*, which also became a film (starring Jason Patric and Jennifer Jason Leigh), draws upon her own experiences as a poorly trained, prematurely immersed narcotics agent at a police department in Texas. In the course of ingratiating herself with drug users in a small town, the book's female protagonist becomes a drug addict herself; to cover for and justify her own misdeeds, she also participates in framing innocent people. Law enforcement has many stories like this. Another, told as a memoir by Joseph Pistone titled *Donnie Brasco* (and as an excellent movie by the same name, starring Johnny Depp and Al Pacino), describes the immersion of FBI agent Pistone in the Bonnano crime family in New York and New Jersey in the years 1976–1981. As he rises in the Mafia, going so far as to become a "made man," Pistone neglects his daughters and his wife, who divorces him. All the while, he is working to gather evidence against the men he spends almost all his time with, over several years, men who think of him like a brother. When he's finished testifying against them, he has to go into witness protection as though he were a mobster-rat himself. While this work may represent a service to the citizenry, I imagine it is seldom a recipe for a happy life.

Late in 2014 the *New York Times* detailed how undercover work has become routine in federal agencies not popularly associated with law enforcement, including the Internal Revenue Service, the

Education Department (where agents of the Office of Inspector General "infiltrate federally funded education programs looking for financial fraud"), the Supreme Court (where security personnel will secretly mingle with protestors outside), and even the Small Business Administration, NASA, and the Smithsonian Institution. The article quoted a former FBI undercover agent who had become a fellow at New York University's law school about whether this was appropriate. Michael German's thoughts might as easily apply to journalism:

> Done right, undercover work can be a very effective law enforcement method, but it carries serious risks and should only be undertaken with proper training, supervision and oversight. Ultimately it is government deceitfulness and participation in criminal activity, which is only justifiable when it is used to resolve the most serious crimes.

Advice for Immersive Writers Considering Undercover Research
Here are some things to keep in mind, many of them suggested by the books I described above.

- Go undercover only with an abundance of caution, and only for a topic important enough to justify the deception.
- Move beyond stunt. Nellie Bly and other reporters of the late nineteenth century weren't called "stunt girls" because they could jump from a galloping horse to a steam train. Rather, they invented eye-catching scenarios that caught readers' attention and sold newspapers. Sometimes this work was lasting and important: Bly's "Ten Days in a Mad-House" was a sensation with public policy ramifications. But other stunts, such as spending the night in a "haunted house," had little relevance to public policy. In our era of

hidden cameras and videos shared on the web, one can "go undercover" at short notice in ways that don't justify it; reputations may suffer unfairly as a result, and deception practiced for trivial matters will feel even worse.

- Endeavor to deceive as little as possible. Lying is a terrible strategy for building relationships. It is also exhausting, and can have legal complications.

- Try hard not to break the law. I did, when I rode the rails (trespassing), to little consequence. But other times it can matter: if your project has an investigatory angle and could earn you enemies, for instance, it's better to keep your conduct legally beyond reproach.

- Do not report surreptitiously from inside your subject's home. Reporting secretly from the workplace is one thing, but entering as a friend into someone's private space is another. Remember Yoram Binur's Palestinian source, angry that he had invited the journalist to sit at his table.

- Do not enter into an intimate relationship with a subject. The way I look at it, intimacy does not exclusively mean having sex; Norah Vincent dated several people who were deceived about her gender. To me, that puts the "pure core" at risk (see below).

- In a related way, do not invade the therapeutic space: do not report from inside self-help groups, whether Alcoholics Anonymous, Gamblers Anonymous, or any other gathering of suffering people who are entrusting their sadness and vulnerability to others in the circle.

- Finally, empathize like there's no tomorrow but also maintain boundaries. What I mean is this: your account of weeks spent with the National Dog-Kickers Association promises to be original and attention-getting. In conversation you've come to see why they act this way, the childhood traumas and low self-esteem that made them mean. But when Friday night rolls around, if you haven't made clear that you're not a kindred soul, you're going to be expected to kick some dogs yourself. This is a bad idea. You might gain acceptance by doing it. But the dogs will feel badly about it immediately, you will feel badly about it, and readers—at least some of them—will dislike you for it when finally your participation is revealed. The lesson: don't go there. Don't do something hurtful that you wouldn't have done as your normal self.

Remember that the reader of your work, whether she's your professor or the guy who saw it in a magazine, becomes complicit in your deception. So in advance, if possible, pause now and then to consider: How will this make me look? Like an empath? Or like an asshole?[*]

Identity & the Pure Core

Mild deception, such as that practiced by the reporters from the *Washington Post* who hung out around Veterans Administration hospitals, is unlikely to make the deceiver lose sleep at night (indeed, if she is performing a public service, she might sleep better!). But let's go toward the opposite end of the spectrum: a writer who enters into an intimate relationship while pretending

---

[*] David Foster Wallace, in a letter to a student of Anne Fadiman's, referred to tone deafness over one's own first-person persona as "the Asshole Problem." In his words, "It's death if the biggest sense the reader gets from a critical essay is that the narrator's a very critical person, or from a comic essay that the narrator's cruel or snooty. Hence the importance of being just as critical about oneself as one is about the stuff/people he's being critical of."

BOX 2. UNDERCOVER, OR JUST DRAWING ON PAST EXPERIENCE?

Sometimes, to expose them to the flavor of undercover reporting, I've sent students out on secret missions. Join a political rally of people you disagree with, I'll say. Attend the weekly services of a religion different than your own. Go to a dealership and price a new top-of-the-line Mercedes. I'll ask them to report back to the class about how they managed, and what it felt like to maintain a secret personal agenda in a social setting. What about it was most difficult? Some will say that the hardest part was simply getting up the nerve. Others might talk about the difficulty of deceiving a particular person (the salesperson, or the contemporary who chatted them up), or of answering a personal question.

What I won't do is ask them to write an article about it because, as I said early in the chapter, I believe that undercover reporting is justified only in certain rare and specific situations.

Now and then, however, a student will ask whether, for an article assignment, they can write about an experience they've *already* had: work as a camp counselor, for example, or volunteering on a suicide helpline. This presents an interesting puzzle. Usually I'll say yes, provided the student meets the two conditions that a magazine would normally ask for:

(1) They protect the privacy of people they were with who didn't expect to appear in a piece of writing. Changing names, and explaining you have done so, is often enough.

(2) They reach out to some of

those same people, and attempt to do some additional reporting. I want them to declare their intention of writing about the experience, in other words, so that their subjects won't be surprised to discover they've been written about, won't feel ambushed.

Some sources will speak only on condition of anonymity. I advise young writers to resist this kind of arrangement when possible. (If they're writing for my class, they have to tell me the source's name.) One solution for getting sources to speak is to decide not to seek to publish. I'm always encouraging my students to publish–it's the way ahead! The way to make a difference! But in those unusual cases where the source is against it, or the student isn't ready for it, keeping the material private can be a way to get it written.

to be someone they're not. Can any public interest justify this? It's hard to think of one.

What I'm getting at is the need to feel good about what you're doing. Is your deception in the service of the good? At the end of the day, will positive results outweigh the negative parts of the process?

It's important to believe they will, because that sense of a worthy cause, of just war, can be essential to psychic survival. It's worth going through a lot if the end result is likely to be something lasting that you're proud of. The only way I know for getting there is to stay clean along the way—to maintain what I call the Pure Core, the self you'll be living with when it's all over. Will that be a self you are proud of for what it's endured? Or a self you're ashamed of for how it stooped? Another way to think of it is Identity Going Forward—how will the future you regard the undercover you? In short, be as scrupulous as possible. Don't kick the dog.

V. WRITING IT

Fiction's first move is imagination; nonfiction's is perception.

JEFF SHARLET, "This Mutant Genre"

George Gudger is a man, et cetera. But obviously, in the effort to tell of him (by example) as truthfully as I can, I am limited. I know him only so far as I know him, and only in those terms in which I know him; and all of that depends as fully on who I am as on who he is.... For that reason and for others, I would do just as badly to simplify or eliminate myself from this picture as to simplify or invent character, places, or atmospheres.

JAMES AGEE, *Let Us Now Praise Famous Men*

Lately I write almost every day. When I was younger, I did not—I'd write when an assignment was due. Back then, one of the most intimidating things in the world to me was the blank sheet of paper, or the empty doc on the computer screen, waiting to be filled.

These days (okay, knock wood) that doesn't often happen. And the reason is because I've learned something over the years: That writing doesn't really begin when you sit down and pick up the pencil. Writing begins before that, when you're doing research, scratching out an outline (it might be a simple list of things you'll touch on), or just thinking. A lot of my writing, as it turns out, gets done on walks, in bed before I get up in the morning, in the bathtub, or during other undemanding moments when I can tap into my subconscious and let my brain organize itself.

Creativity, I mentioned earlier, is indispensable in nonfiction writing. Brainstorming a topic, devising a way to gain access, and research itself are all creative acts. The most effective research anticipates that which will be written: it looks for story, and tries to imagine form: where will it begin, where will it go, how will it end? If you've given these things some thought before you sit down to write, the writing will be easier.

THE NARRATOR

Sometimes, in the course of a long project, someone will ask me, "Can you start writing before your research is done?" Generally the answer is no. I can't bake a cake before I know which ingredients I'll have at my disposal, or how much of each one. Baking is all about relative proportions; in this sense so is writing. In general, research has to be completed before the writing can begin.

That is not to say that you shouldn't practice along the way, try some things out. Writing a few scenes or sketching a character can help you recognize the story that's there, and ultimately organize it. If the story you discover in your sketching is different from what you expected, you can redirect your research in order to get what you need. Long narratives are hard, and hard to conceive all at once. There are different ways to get there and one usually has to shake off false leads and dead ends and keep an open mind until it all comes together.

That said, at some point a writer needs to end the research phase and begin to write; and the easiest way to make the transition is to have some degree of confidence that you know most of what you need to in order to write it.

With my first book, *Rolling Nowhere*, I did not follow this process because I had frankly never dreamed that the experience would one day become a book. Rather, I had researched a third-person undergraduate anthropology thesis, which was a very different end point. After my travel was over, and while I was writing my thesis—a few weeks afterwards—I thought about all the interesting things I was having to leave out because they were about my immersion and therefore personal to me: the enhanced importance of brushing my teeth during my field work, for example (good teeth were a discreet dividing line between me and real hoboes, and I didn't want to lose them), or the new experience of being ignored or avoided by attractive women my own age (tramps might have been used to that, but I wasn't). I kept a growing file of everything of significance that didn't fit into my thesis and by and by I concluded that yes, there was another thing I could write from all of this: a first-person story for which I'd need to reorganize all the notes I had taken in the service of writing the thesis.

To write the book that became Coyotes, the process was frankly easier because I had done something similar already. I knew I would need to spend months with migrants, and get to know a number of them well. I suspected that one way to do this would be to spend time with them not only in the United States, where they were working, but back home in Mexico, where they came from. In addition, it seemed kind of clear to me that I should cross the border in the company of some of these folks. In terms of the narrative I would tell, that passage had real and also symbolic meaning—symbolic in that it was an action that widely helped define the subject. You left home and crossed into another country without permission: that action helped define the class of people who were my subjects. So it made sense that I would want to see that firsthand, and take part in it if possible. (The comparable central, symbolic action of a book about hoboes, it seemed to me, was hopping a freight train. Doing that, in a certain way, defined the person I was writing about.) In both cases, I needed stories of those things. When I contemplated writing a book from my hobo field notes, I knew (retrospectively) that element was very much present. When I contemplated writing a book about migrants, I knew (prospectively/proactively) that such an element really should be part of my research: I needed to cross the border in the company of undocumented migrants. Much of my research followed organically from that: A crossing would give me reason to visit (or live in) the town where the crossers came from. After crossing, I would want to see (and possibly get hired by) at least one of the places where they work. And on and on.

And after my experience with Rolling Nowhere, I knew, as I conducted research, that one of the things I was taking notes about was my own first-person experience. So I broadened my notes to include aspects of a personal diary: how it felt today when X said Y, or what a revelation it was when A told me B, or how unequipped I was to handle Z. Because those things, as much as ethnographic insights, would matter to the readers of the kind of first-person book I had in mind (and might even matter more than the other things).

Who Is Speaking, and to Whom?

Writing Rolling Nowhere was difficult; I got blocked several times. At one point I flew to New York and talked about it with Rich Barber, the editor at Viking Press who had acquired my (as yet unwritten) book on the basis of a proposal. That conversation helped me to understand that, up to that point in my life, I'd always known who I was writing something *for* . . . lately it had been professors. Now who was it, I asked him—editors?

No, said Rich. Write it for a friend. Write it for a close friend, one who has been away since before you even had the idea of riding the rails. You've invited this friend over for dinner and maybe you've opened a bottle of wine. This person totally means it when he says, *okay, so tell me everything,* and when he learns that means hours of listening lie ahead, he's actually glad. Write it for him: tell him the story.

When I got home and tried that, everything became much easier.

Explaining my*self*—who I am, why I did a thing like ride the rails—was not terribly difficult with *Rolling Nowhere*, perhaps because I'd been having to do it out loud, with family and friends, for months before I sat down to write a book. But that's not always the case. Often, if not usually, questions can accompany an author's choice of subject and his relationship to it. If he is a character in the story, these questions become even more significant; readers will be judging the author on the basis of how he presents himself in the story.

Vivian Gornick analyzes some challenges of first-person narration in the thoughtful introduction to *The Situation and the Story: The Art of Personal Narrative*. One of her most illuminating observations concerns the special nature of a nonfiction narrator. In fiction, Gornick observes, a narrator can be unreliable—he can lie or distort in ways that are interesting. But not in nonfiction writing. A first-person narrator in nonfiction writing must convince the reader that he is truthful and forthcoming.

That might seem to make things simpler, except for one thing: even this honest nonfiction narrator is actually a persona. He is one *side* of the author, the person telling the story. In other words, each of us has many sides. We act and speak one way as a parent, another way as a child, another way as a friend, perhaps another way as a partner in a romantic relationship. The letters we might write while inhabiting each of these roles would likely show different but important differences in tone.

Gornick asserts that the writer needs to figure out which part of herself is speaking when she tells a story. Her book opens with the example of a eulogy delivered at a memorial service for a pioneering doctor. Of many speakers, only a woman who had been the doctor's student "moved me to that melancholy evocation of world-and-self that makes a single person's death feel large," and the student focused on their particular relationship in her remarks. The memory of "coming under the formative influence" of the deceased had acted as an organizing principle that determined the structure of her remarks.

Structure had imposed order. Order made the sentences more shapely. Shapeliness increased the expressiveness of the language. Expressiveness deepened association. At last, a dramatic buildup occurred, one that had layered into it the descriptive feel of a young person's apprenticeship, medical practices in a time of social change, and a divided attachment to a mentor who could bring herself only to correct, never to praise. This buildup is called texture. It was the texture that had stirred me; caused me to feel, with powerful immediacy, not only the actuality of the woman being remembered but — even more vividly — the presence of the one doing the remembering . . .

The better the speaker imagined herself, the more vividly she brought the dead doctor to life. . . . Of the various selves at her disposal (she was, after all, many people — a daughter, a lover, a bird-watcher, a New Yorker), she knew and didn't forget that the only proper self to invoke was the one that had been apprenticed.

Narrative persona in first-person nonfiction is thus another way of saying "choice of selves." Or, who's talking? (When I showed my agent the first draft of my proposal for this book, she said something to the effect of, this part sounds a little bit like a professor giving a lecture. That wasn't what I was after, so I retooled.) The more personal the first-person narration, the more key this choice becomes. In the kinds of personal essay Gornick is describing, the persona is no less than the "instrument of illumination." Who are you in relation to your story?

vvv

A concept that comes up a lot in reported writing but particularly in immersive projects is distance, as in "I need a little time to get some distance on things." You've been close to it and need to step away in order to gain perspective, figure out *what matters about this to everyday people?* This can be another way of saying you've moved too near the Participant end of the Participant-Observer spectrum, and need to move back toward Observer. Typically one does this by de-immersing—going home, visiting family, seeing old friends. Or, as mentioned above, by inviting that old friend over for dinner and having an extended debriefing session or two. You'll hear a different person speaking, in these sessions, than the one you were when immersed. This different person, in my experience, is the one who will be telling the story in writing.

An extreme version of this apparently applies to one of my favorite works of immersion writing, Stanley Booth's *Dance with the Devil: The Rolling Stones and Their Times*. Booth, who had written a profile of an old-time blues musician from Memphis known as Furry Lewis, signed an agreement with the Stones in 1969 to travel with the band and write a book about it. The experience, filled with drugs, sex, and constant travel around one of culture's hottest flames, utterly consumed him; his book did not appear until 1984. My new editor at Random House (I had switched publishing houses, from Viking, for *Coyotes*) was also Booth's editor, and handed me a copy of the book when it came out. I asked him why it had taken so long; he grimaced and said, "long story." The book sold little but endured; at least two editions since have kept it alive, and garnered a wide circle of admirers. In a new afterword to the 2000 edition, Booth tried to explain the delay.

I had to become a different person from the narrator in order to tell the story. This was necessary because of the heartbreak, the disappointment, the chagrin, the regret, the remorse. We had all, Stones, fans, hangers-on, parasites, observers, been filled with optimism there in the autumn of 1969 . . . we believed that we were different, that we were somehow chosen, or anointed, for success, for love and happiness. We were wrong.

Elsewhere in the afterword, he writes that he had to overcome depression and "domestic upheaval."

So torn was I that at times I begged for death and for years tempted death almost constantly, at last throwing myself off a North Georgia mountain waterfall onto the granite boulders below, smashing my face, breaking my back.

A cynical reader might wonder if such a talented writer simply required a dramatic explanation—for himself, as much as anyone—for his book being nearly fifteen years late. On the other hand, perhaps journalism approaching this level of art might necessarily exact such a price: If you take Booth's explanation at face value, his time with the Stones becomes a kind of parable about participatory journalism. The book was a standout because Booth involved himself so fully not just in a band tour but also in the passions of a generation. And yet, as the world changed, there was no way for that participant to write the book until he became somebody else and could look back on his experience as a thing apart, something that happened to a different person in a time long past. Either way, Booth's afterword brings me a bit closer to solving the question I asked my editor those many years ago, about what took the book so long to come out. I don't think he knew the answer, anyway.

BOX 3: LEGAL TROUBLE

Nobody wants legal trouble. But sometimes writing occasions it, particularly if the writer is famous or a book has sold a lot of copies or contains intimate revelations. Susanna Kaysen, known for *Girl, Interrupted*, was sued over a later memoir. Her boyfriend, she said without naming him, had been cruel and abusive in bed. He said this was untrue and sued for invasion of privacy. Kathryn Stockett, author of the bestselling novel *The Help*, was sued by an elderly former housekeeper who claimed a main character was based on her. The journalist Dale Maharidge and his coauthor, photographer Michael Williamson, were sued by a subject after their book won the Pulitzer Prize; she claimed that they had promised to share proceeds with her.

None of those lawsuits was successful; United States law offers fairly broad protections to writers. Still, just getting sued can be expensive and stressful. And laws in other countries differ significantly from our own. While I am not lawyer, I can tell you about suggestions that some smart lawyers have made to me over the years.

Listen to your editor. Good editors can help writers avoid common pitfalls. Oftentimes, they work in concert with attorneys to offer writers advice. This is true with periodicals as well as with book publishers: each of my immersion books has had a legal review that resulted in my being asked several questions. And several times my editors have asked counsel to look over nearly finished articles prior to publication. Some questions I remember from over the years:

- *Does the fact he was smoking marijuana appear in your original notes?* (Answer: yes, it does.)
- *Did he have a permit for the pistol you describe in his possession?* (Answer, supplied after some research: No, but that state did not require a permit for one.)
- *Did you tell the truth on the job application?* (Answer: yes, and I made a copy before I sent it in.)
- *Some of these men you name were convicted of crimes. You name others who were with them but not convicted—would it be okay to remove their names from the article?* (Answer: yes. I did not want to imply guilt by association.)

Get releases. Sometimes publishers will direct writers to ask their subjects to sign a "model release" giving the writer permission to use the stories of their private lives, quotations, and sometimes photographs, and making clear they do not expect anything in return. I have never been asked to do this—but Dale Maharidge, mentioned above, was. Upon being sued, he showed it to the plaintiff's lawyer and . . . end of lawsuit.

No publisher? Check with a lawyer. The writers at greatest risk of being sued, some experts say, are those who post intimate details of the lives of friends or acquaintances who are not public figures on Facebook, blogs, or elsewhere online. Posting can be considered publishing; old-fashioned legal risks live on in the digital age. If in doubt, talk to an attorney with experience in publishing. Some have posted at www.writersdigest.com and www.rightsofwriters.com; you can search for Volunteer Lawyers for the Arts or the Legal Defense Hotline of the Report ers Committee for Freedom of the Press.

Be scrupulous and fair. Many publishing lawsuits seem to be less about greed than about feelings of anger and betrayal. The day she opened the magazine or web page, the subject of the writing felt blindsided or humiliated, treated unfairly, stabbed in the back. Could some of these reactions have been anticipated over the course of the long reporting experiences typical of immersion writing, and possibly headed off? Sometimes, maybe. There is, in any event, a short list of common sense measures a writer can take in hopes of inoculating himself against lawsuits:

- Be scrupulous with intimate details of others' lives. Make sure what you say is accurate: back up statements with evidence. Consider presenting unflattering information as your considered opinion, rather than as hard fact.

- Anonymize to protect privacy. In some cases, anonymizing is bad journalism: Journalists covering the news need to name names, and better publications will insist on it. In feature writing, though, when a story has been researched among people who are not otherwise in the news, anonymizing can make good journalism possible. Writers should protect the privacy of children and of others who wish to maintain it. And people who have been observed surreptitiously, such as the meat inspectors and correction officers I worked alongside in different projects, should be given the option of having their privacy protected.

- Communicate criticism before publication to minimize a subject's surprise; make clear your differences in advance. In other words, don't shy from disagreement or (civilized) argument during research, saving your punches for publication when the subject can't fight back.

• Aim to treat even those you may be critical of with respect.

STRUCTURE

Tolstoy is often credited with saying, "All great literature is one of two stories; a man goes on a journey or a stranger comes to town," and it's largely true. There are main characters, who come to be at cross-purposes. Their intensifying conflict ("rising action") drives the story, and readers' interest. It peaks at the climax, after which there is resolution, and denouement ("falling action"). My high school English teacher liked to represent this graphically, with a "narrative arc" on the chalkboard. Traditional narratives have a plot, in which one action leads to another, and they have scenes.

Narratives of the nonfiction variety often have many of these elements but seldom have them all. That is because assembling them is just too difficult; real life just doesn't often serve up stories in the conventional form, especially the cause-and-effect chain that adds up to plot. On the other hand, real life can often supply an element that fiction lacks, which is believability, and relevance to everyday life: nonfiction writers get to say *this really happened*.

The two elements of traditional narrative that most often play a part in nonfiction narratives are character and scene. We tend to write about people; take a source and turn him into a multidimensional person and you have the beginnings of a character;

add the idea of desire and show that person pursuing his goal, and you have a more complete character. Put that character in a room, or in a car, or on a mountainside, with something happening, and you have a scene. Better scenes have something happening in them, and the best tend to have conflict: the officer is demanding a bribe, the girl is saying no, the company is making money but there's a cost. And it is possible to have dialogue, an enjoyable element of so many stories. Often, though, in nonfiction the exchanges will be brief, as it can be difficult for the reporter to predict and record key conversations.

Below we'll look at the structure of several books to see how the authors used narrative. But I should stress that narrative can also be deployed in articles. Long pieces such as Amy Harmon's "Navigating Love and Autism," about the romance between two college-age students with autism, or Matthew Power's "Mississippi Drift: River Vagrants in the Age of Wal-Mart," are full-fledged narratives that read like fiction. They have beginnings, middles, and ends, conflicts and resolutions, scenes and characters.

Importantly, a piece can still be narrative and not have all those elements. Susan Orlean's classic article for Esquire, "The American Man, Age Ten," interweaves scenes with sections of exposition. She shows her 10-year-old protagonist, Colin Duffy, in his fifth-grade classroom, in a pizzeria playing Nintendo with a friend, at home in his room, and finally, at dusk, in his backyard. There is no progression or chronology, per se, but the depiction of Duffy is delightful, even spellbinding. It goes to show that writing doesn't have to be purely narrative; it can be partly narrative. Narrative can be a question of degree.

One of the most stripped-down uses of narrative is bookending. In this strategy, an article (and it may be a short article) will begin with a scene and end with a scene, and in between will be exposition. Sometimes, in fact, the beginning scene and ending scene are part of the same scene, which is interrupted by the exposition. I recommend Jack Hart's *Storycraft: The Complete Guide to Writing Narrative Nonfiction* to would-be immersion writers looking for detailed advice on using narrative in articles brief and lengthy.

vvv

Every nonfiction book is different, of course, and every nonfiction story is told in a different way. For the purposes of this book, I'd like to focus mainly on structure, as in my experience it seems to be the most vexing element for developing writers. I'll discuss a handful of books of immersion writing, to show the variety of possible successful storytelling strategies.

A central question is how to handle chronology. In every story, time passes and things happen. But though time is linear, there are many ways to present it.

The most boring is a dutiful recounting of days or weeks with equal weight given to everything that happened. As a boy, I remember my growing impatience with the slideshows that friends and neighbors would host upon return from trips overseas, with their plodding presentation of the monumental and the expected: Sure, the pyramids are cool but tell us about the day you lost your wallet. Did you taste a new flavor in all those days? Did you see a sight—a beggar, a demonstration, a work of art—that you can't get out of your mind? Did you have trouble focusing on the present because of news from home? What local person did you come to know the best?

The passage of time, to be interesting, must be massaged. Certain eventful minutes may be expanded in the telling, and fill paragraphs. But the reader will be grateful if less eventful minutes, even days or weeks, are ignored. A timeline must be stretched and compressed until it *serves the story*.

Similarly, timelines can be stepped out of, or artistically rearranged. *In medias res* is Latin for "in the middle of things"; a story which uses *in medias res* opens somewhere other than the beginning, often in the midst of action. It's a way of getting the reader's attention that is centuries old (*Hamlet* opens after the death of Hamlet's father, the king; *Paradise Lost* begins with Satan already in hell). Exposition that explains how we got here can be added later. The classic film *Sunset Boulevard* famously opens with the last thing that happens: police find a well-dressed body floating facedown in a swimming pool. How did it get there?

Chronological storytelling can also be interrupted with digressions—a brief story-within-a-story, or a bit of background or exposition that adds meaning to the action. A digression can tell us about the history of a place or of a relationship. If the narration is first-person, it might fill in something important about the storyteller's own background or connection to the story. Storytellers must always be mindful of the cost of digression, however: the risk of losing a reader's interest, rather than piquing it.

An excellent way to educate oneself about structure is to read, watch, or listen to a story twice—the first time for pleasure, and the second time to see how it was done. Paying attention to structure might not be as fun, but it's the way to become a writer: the masters' secrets are right in front of us, if only we take the time to appreciate their craftsmanship.

In medias res

Examples abound of nonfiction stories that begin *in medias res*. Take Plimpton's *Paper Lion*, which opens with the writer, 36, heading to Detroit Lions pre-season training camp in 1963. That's the first of 30 short chapters. The second chapter takes readers back in time to his efforts to find a team to join. After much trying, he wrangles from the Lions an invitation to their three-week training camp in July. It's not revealed then, but he'll eventually get to throw some passes in an intra-squad game in early August, and then sit on the bench at an exhibition game against the Cleveland Browns a week later.

Some 25 years later, H. G. "Buzz" Bissinger also wrote about football—but in a completely different way. His bestselling *Friday Night Lights: A Town, A Team, and a Dream*, which inspired the movie and hit television series of the same name, recounts one momentous season in the life of a team in small-town Texas. The bulk of the book proceeds chronologically through three main sections: Pre-Season (46 pages), The Season (134 pages), Push For the Playoffs (53 pages), and the Post-Season (70 pages). But the book's Prologue extracts a moment from late in the season—a handful of key players and the coach prepare for a game against an archrival for the district championship—and moves it up front, providing readers with an exciting foreshadowing of where this all is going. (Bissinger, unlike Plimpton, leaves himself out of the story.)

Krakauer's *Into Thin Air: A Personal Account of the Mount Everest Disaster* tells the story of an adventure that turned into a headline-making tragedy. Following a brief introduction, which reveals that four of Krakauer's climbing mates, including the main guide, will soon perish, the book opens with Krakauer summiting the world's highest peak. But the moment is hardly triumphal. A longtime climber with noncommercial values, Krakauer is part of a commercial expedition to Mount Everest. People on these expeditions pay a lot for extraordinary assistance that gives them a reasonable chance of making the top. Once there, muddy-headed from the elevation and with a big storm moving in, Krakauer heads back down almost immediately. End of chapter.

Chapter 2 then takes us all the way back to 1852 and the discovery of Everest as the highest place on the planet, a mountain whose heights were "foreign to all experience." In 1924 a British team including George Leigh Mallory attempted to climb Everest; Mallory is famous for having answered a question about why with the words, "because it's there." Partway up the mountain, he and his climbing partner disappeared and were never seen again. Sir Edmund Hillary and Tenzing Norgay succeeded in making the top "a month before I was conceived." Everest remained a top trophy among climbers until billionaire Dick Bass, with considerable help, summited in 1985, which "rudely pulled Everest into the postmodern era." By chapter's end, *Outside* magazine has assigned Krakauer to accompany one of the proliferating commercial climbs of Everest, and take part in a phenomenon which he sees as profaning something sacred.

Set not terribly far away, but depicting an utterly different world, is Katherine Boo's award-winning *Behind the Beautiful Forevers: Life, Death, and Hope in a Mumbai Undercity*, about life in a slum. The book opens with a main character, a young junk collector named Abdul, fleeing home because he's been falsely accused of helping drive his next-door neighbor, the One-Leg, to suicide. Abdul's hiding place is behind cans and other recyclables in a dark shed attached to his family's house. The actual accusation against him isn't leveled until page 96 (out of 256 pages). A few pages later, Abdul, his father, and sister are arrested. The book ends with the judge's verdict in the criminal cases against them.

I have begun three books, and many long articles, *in medias res*. *Rolling Nowhere* opens with my trying to catch a freight train out of St. Louis, Missouri, which seemed to me the first step into the hoboes' world. "I crouched quietly in the patch of tall weeds," is the first sentence. The chapter ends just a few paragraphs later with my elation at succeeding after some failed attempts. Chapter 2 begins, "The other reasons [I wanted to hop a train] I never found easy to explain," and then goes back in time in search of motivations. Chapter 3 picks up the narrative begun in chapter 1, recounting the first successful ride of my journey.

I rewrote the first chapter of *Newjack* at least a dozen times. After the first seven or eight left me still unsatisfied, I abandoned the effort for a while and jumped into the *chronological* beginning of my story, which was, after some short background, my arrival at the corrections training academy. But I didn't think that was where I wanted to begin the book. Rather I wanted to bring a reader immediately into Sing Sing prison with me, a rookie officer.

Only half a dozen people knew about my book at this point; I had successfully kept it a secret for more than a year. One of those people, a good friend, had figured it out one evening when I'd called him from a pay phone inside the prison line-up room, and he had heard my coworkers shouting to me in the background. I was relieved he knew, actually, because I needed advice. How should I begin? I asked him.

Steve, a documentary filmmaker, said if it were a movie he'd begin like this: describe arriving at work, first in the parking lot, then in the locker room and line-up room, and then in the housing block where I spent most days. "Take the reader inside with you, like there's a camera on your shoulder," he suggested. So that's what I tried with my next draft, and I loved the result. After only three more rewrites, I was essentially done with the first chapter. The second chapter begins with my idea for the project, and everything up to arriving at the training academy.

Narrative magazine articles can be started the same way, in *medias res*. So it was with "The Hand-Off," my *New York Times Magazine* article about AIDS orphans.

Early in the AIDS epidemic, before the advent of anti-retroviral drugs, it was thought that the spread of the disease to women could result in an epidemic of orphans. I wrote about an early effort to connect a sick mom with a potential adoptive mom: somebody who could replace her. It was dramatic material. The future orphan, only eleven years old at the time, had trouble expressing her feelings directly but her mom gave me a letter the girl wrote to Santa Claus, asking for someone to take care of her once her mom couldn't. I opened my narrative with that letter, and a three-paragraph introduction of Christy, her mother Evelyn, and their predicament. After a space break, I offered seven paragraphs of background on AIDS and the growing problem of orphans. After another space break I returned to the narrative of Christy and her mom, going back to the behavior that she thought had gotten her sick, attempts to find a relative who might step in, and other background. About a third of the way in I caught up to the present day, with Christy and Evelyn trying to make up their minds about a prospective adoptive mother they had been put in touch with by an adoption agency. The first part of my story I didn't witness; it was recounted to me by those who were in it. The second part I mainly got to see myself.

Straight Chronology

Other times it works best just to start at the beginning and continue to the end. A common temporal frame for a book-length project is one year. Tracy Kidder's wonderful *Among Schoolchildren* (1989) describes a year in the fifth-grade classroom of public school teacher Chris Zajac in Holyoke, Massachusetts. Chapters proceed chronologically from the first, "September," to the last, "June," but intermediate chapters have titles such as "Homework," "Discipline," "Sent Away" (about a single troubled child), and "Science Fair." Each is broken into smaller parts—three sections in "September," eight in "Sent Away." Though he basically sat in the classroom for a year, Kidder leaves himself out of the story. His characters are the teacher and her students. The first paragraph of the book is a lovely example of how a great writer can be creative while adhering to traditional chronological storytelling:

> Mrs. Zajac wasn't born yesterday. She knows you didn't do your best work on this paper, Clarence. Don't you remember Mrs. Zajac saying that if you didn't do your best, she'd make you do it over? As for you, Claude, God forbid that you should ever need brain surgery. But Mrs. Zajac hopes that if you do, the doctor won't open up your head and walk off saying he's almost done, as you just said when Mrs. Zajac asked you for your penmanship, which, by the way, looks like who did it and ran. Felipe, the reason you have hiccups is, your mouth is always open and the wind rushes in. You're in fifth grade now. So, Felipe, put a lock on it. Zip it up. Then go get a drink of water.

Alex Kotlowitz framed *There Are No Children Here* in a period of just over two years, and used straight chronology. A preface recalls how he met the brothers and their mother, LaJoe, at a shoot for a photo essay on children in poverty for *Chicago* magazine. The memory of the meeting stuck with him; nobody should be living as they did, he thought, in the gang-ridden public housing behemoth called the Henry Horner Homes. He returned a couple of years later as a reporter for the *Wall Street Journal* for a story focused on inner-city violence; the year after that, he suggested to LaJoe that he write a book about her family, and especially the boys.

It's an intimate, measured, and often painful tale about two likable kids in a scary world. "If I grow up, I'd like to be a bus driver," Lafeyette, then ten, told Kotlowitz. "*If*, not *when*," observes the author. "At the age of ten, Lafeyette wasn't sure he'd make it to adulthood." As the reader sees the courses the boys' lives take over the coming months and years, the reader isn't too sure, either.

Kotlowitz divides the book into seasons (Summer 1987, Fall 1987-Spring 1988, etc.), and shifts his focus between the boys, their mother, and events in the neighborhood. After the preface, he sticks to the third person until the epilogue and "A Note on Reporting Methods" at the end.

Adrian LeBlanc's epic *Random Family* begins a year or two before the trial of a heroin kingpin known as Boy George. LeBlanc, who decided to follow the life of the kingpin's girlfriend, Jessica, after he was convicted, had to report that earlier period of Jessica's life in retrospect, not firsthand. But by spending days, weeks, months, and years with Jessica, her friend Coco, and others, and checking in constantly, she achieves a convincing re-creation. Following Boy George's conviction, Jessica, who briefly worked in one of his heroin mills, is sent to prison too. But his life sentence overshadows her sentence of ten years; she gets out after seven and resumes her life, with new partners, children, a move upstate—but throughout has an unswerving friendship with Coco, whose life involves a version of the same. The book's 44 chapters, organized into five sections, reflect chapters of the women's lives; the sections are, in order: The Street, Lockdown, Upstate, House to House, and Breaking Out.

Immersive nonfiction need not be urban and gritty. Joe Mackall became interested in the Amish simply because he lived near them, in rural Ohio. Down the street, an Amish family moved into an "English" (non-Amish) house and promptly de-Englished it, building an outhouse and setting the toilet out in the garbage, for example. Six months later Mackall asked the father, Samuel, whether he might board his daughter's horse. Thus began a relationship that grew closer when Mackall learned that Samuel's mother had died, in Canada, the same week Samuel's wife was due to give birth. Mackall offered to drive him 500 miles to the funeral (since Amish don't drive), and then turn right around and drive him back. Samuel asked his bishop for permission, and they were off.

That's how *Plain Secrets* begins; the bulk of it transpires ten years after. By then Mackall (who tells the story in a modest first person) has discovered that his neighbors are Swartzentruber Amish, the most conservative of several Amish sects in North America. And that they are beset, like other orthodox, with defections from the faith, including a nephew whom Mackall gets to know. Mackall rides in Samuel's horse-drawn buggy (extremely dangerous at night, when cars don't see it) and sees the family mourn a 9-year-old daughter who dies of a brain tumor. It's an ideal set-up for first-person narration, which the author handles with aplomb.

By Theme
The writer Sebastian Junger, best known for his book *The Perfect Storm* and for war reporting from around the world, made five visits to Afghanistan's Korengal Valley over a year, starting in June 2007. His idea was to visit an extreme outpost of the American military and portray the lives of soldiers there, soldiers who engaged in frequent combat. What he saw, up close, was amazing— soldiers mustering courage, soldiers dealing with loss, soldiers living under constant threat of attack. From their mountaintop post, nicknamed Restrepo after a soldier who had died there, the company made forays down into the valley, where enemy combatants tried to kill them, and sometimes succeeded.

There was just one problem, when it came to knitting his reports for *Vanity Fair* (which sponsored his travel) into a book: the soldiers didn't stay at Restrepo for a whole year. In fact, it often seems, reading the book closely, that there was little continuity, soldier-wise, from one visit to the next. The *place* was a constant, but the *characters* changed.

"I was desperate for an organizing idea that wasn't chronological," Junger told a class of my graduate students in 2015. His solution was to overlay a roughly chronological story with a thematic one. *War* is divided into three sections, each labeled with a theme. Book One is called "Fear." Book Two is "Killing," and Book Three is "Love." The minimalistic labels are of a piece with the book's title; together they seem to encourage us to consider big ideas, general themes, and outlines, more than a very specific story.

The book starts with Junger's arrival in Afghanistan, and ends with his departure, but departs from chronology in some of the telling. There are digressions, into a visit by a soldier to Junger's place in New York, into ideas of courage in literature, into what was happening back home for some of the characters. Basically it all holds together, due, I'd say, in equal measure to the strength of Junger's material, and his skills as a storyteller.

Other Structures

Lis Harris' *Holy Days: The World of the Hasidic Family* also had its beginning as a series of magazine articles—for the *New Yorker*, where Harris was a staff writer. An immersion into the world of Hasidic Jews of the Lubavitcher sect in Crown Heights, Brooklyn, it opens with Harris recalling looking at a stack of family photos that included one of "a fierce-looking, bearded old man, wearing the sort of fur hat and long black coat that Hasidic men wear. When I asked my mother (a Manhattan-bred lawyer) who he was, she peered at the photograph briefly and disapprovingly and shrugged, 'Nobody in our family.'" Today's secular Jews find the existence of Hasidim mildly embarrassing, in Harris' telling, but she wonders if perhaps her mother was wrong: "Our progenitors came from Austria, Romania, and Russia, and in the nineteenth century, three quarters of the Jewish population of Eastern Europe was Hasidic." Harris describes her family's attitude toward their Jewishness as "more or less that of fans whose home team was the Jews." But she is curious and wants to understand her connection, if any, to this antique strand of her family tree, living insular lives in modern-day Brooklyn. This question about her connection to the Luba-vitchers is a low-key leitmotif of Holy Days, and one of the things that binds its chapters together.

The other thing is an emphasis on religious holidays: To a great extent, Harris organized her book in the way her subjects organize their lives. Holy Days, though researched over several years, follows Lubavitchers over the course of one, in which she joins the community as it celebrates Passover, Rosh Hashanah and Yom Kippur, and Succoth. Her main link is a woman she calls Sheina Konigsberg and her family, a husband (a widower), and his two sons and three daughters from a previous marriage. Sometimes she's with the group but other times she's with only Sheina, for example at one of the lengthy Shabbos services at the sect's headquarters on Eastern Parkway, where men and women listened separately to the group's beloved leader of the time, Rebbe Menachem Schneerson. In between the holidays are chapters with little or no reference to the family, such as two about the history of Hasidic dynasties, one about a rival Hasidic group, and one about dissidents who leave the fold. Unlike either kind is a particularly affecting chapter in which Sheina shows Harris a new community mikvah, or ritual bath, that she helped establish. It is in the mikvah, alone with a female attendant, that Harris literally immerses herself. "The second time down, I see a little speeded-up movie of all the religious people I know, performing this ritual. I think of all the generations of people I have not known who have considered the impurities of the world dissolvable.... The third time down, I think of my boys suspended inside me, waiting to join the world."

The passage is all the more striking because of how sparing

Harris is with personal details throughout. This is no "journey of self-discovery" ("I wasn't searching for my roots," Harris explained to me) but rather a probing look at a vibrant group of people the author refused to write off as antique or unknowable.

By choosing to write about the Hmong, Anne Fadiman faced a challenge possibly greater than Harris' or Mackall's: readers might have heard of Hasidim or the Amish, but few even knew how to pronounce Hmong (close your lips, blow a wisp of air out your nose, and say "mong"). To make us care, Fadiman needed to do a lot of explaining . . . but too much explaining can slow a story down. Her solution involved a number of creative strategies, among them recreating scenes that she herself had not witnessed, but the details of which she researched exhaustively. The book begins, for instance, like this:

If Lia Lee had been born in the highlands of northwest Laos, where her parents and twelve of her brothers and sisters were born, her mother would have squatted on the floor of the house that her father had built from ax-hewn planks thatched with bamboo and grass. The floor was dirt, but it was clean. Her mother, Foua, sprinkled it regularly with water to keep the dust down and swept it every morning and evening with a broom she had made of grass and bark. She used a bamboo dustpan, which she had also made herself, to collect the feces of the children who were too young to defecate outside, and emptied its contents in the forest. Even if Foua had been a less fastidious housekeeper, her newborn babies wouldn't have gotten dirty, since she never let them actually touch the floor. She remains proud to this day that she delivered each of them into her own hands, reaching between her legs to ease out the head and then letting the rest of the body slip out onto her bent forearms.

Afterwards, Foua would bury the placenta under that dirt floor. This opening sets the stage for one kind of existence meeting another: How do you give birth, and where do you bury the placenta, when you live in a carpeted apartment in Merced, California? And how do you treat your daughter's epilepsy, which back home is considered a spiritual gift, as it gets more and more severe? Fadiman presents the Hmong as not inscrutable but fascinating, and her enthusiasm becomes infectious. She manages the exposition by alternating narrative chapters with expository ones, including history of the Hmong before they fled southern China for Laos; how they supported the United States during the Vietnam war, when the CIA funded their insurgency; and how they responded to Western medicine in refugee camps in Thailand. Though Fadiman drew heavily on ethnographies of the Hmong—her bibliography is chock-full of them—she did not want to write one. "A Venn diagram of subject matter" for her book and Hmong ethnographies "was almost a complete overlap," she told my graduate students in 2015. "But a Venn diagram of approaches and style was two separate circles."[*]

It was not until my second reading of the book that I realized the author had not been present during the early months of Lia's illness. Rather, she reconstructed it, using medical records and interviews with medical staff, family, social workers, and anyone else she could find with knowledge. Reconstructing scenes is a risky business, because the temptation to take liberties is great: a lesser writer might have imagined quotations, or the thoughts of

[*] Amy Harmon, the Pulitzer-winning *New York Times* writer of science-themed narratives, told my class that her goal, when possible, is to have a story explain itself, to have "argument without explication" that minimizes exposition. Her long article, "Navigating Love and Autism," also recounts many scenes from early in her subjects' relationship, before Harmon had met them.

main characters, thus veering into fiction. But Fadiman is rigorous, and that saves her.

It also helps that she leavens her rigor with humor. Despite the gravity of the situation and all that is at stake, Fadiman enjoys retelling Hmong folk tales about *dabs*, or evil spirits, that have funny morals, and includes passages like this:

> Meeting a Hmong is like getting into a speakeasy: everything depends on who sent you. My appointment with the Lees had been arranged by Blia Yao Moua ... a man fortuitously unconnected to the hospital or any other American institution. What's more, May Ying's [her interpreter's] husband, Pheng, belong to the same clan as the Lees ... which led Foua and Nao Kao to treat [her] like a long-lost niece. Within thirty seconds, I could see I was dealing with a family that bore little resemblance to the one the doctors had described. The Lees struck me as smart, humorous, talkative, and energetic. I wish I could say it was my skill as an interviewer that brought out these excellent qualities. In truth, I repeatedly embarrassed May Ying by asking her to translate questions of such surpassing ignorance that after I got to know the Lees I began to feel my primary role in their household was as a source of mirth. May Ying referred to these questions ("Did you bury your children's placentas?" "In Laos, were there a lot of *dabs* who lived in the rivers, lakes, and trees?" "Do you sacrifice pigs?") as my "Is the Pope Catholic?" questions because any fool would know the answers were yes. Once, when I asked in which part of their house in Laos the family had relieved themselves, Foua laughed so hard she almost fell off her bamboo stool. "In the forest, of course!" she finally gasped, tears running down her cheeks.

A book structured differently from any of the above—and written and conceived *very* differently—is also one of the most recent, as of this writing: Jennifer Percy's *Demon Camp: A Soldier's Exorcism*. On one level, Percy's book is about posttraumatic stress disorder. But only occasionally does Percy step back to the "issues" level. Mainly her project is to get close up and render the subjective reality of her subject, Sgt. Caleb Daniels, as vividly as possible.

Daniels, a helicopter gunner who did several tours of duty with the Army in Afghanistan, is haunted by the death of his crewmates aboard a MH-47 Chinook, shot down by a rocket-propelled grenade during a rescue mission that he was not on. Percy got to know Daniels over three years of visits to his home in Georgia while she was a student in the nonfiction MFA program of the University of Iowa. The first part of her book describes Daniels, the history of his military service, and his vivid experience of nighttime visits by a presence he calls the Black Thing and believes to be an actual demon. Though writing in the third person, Percy aims to capture Daniels' *subjective* reality: never is the existence of this demon questioned, or explained as a symptom of trauma.

With part II, on page 49, Percy switches to the first person, and an account of Daniels' current life. (Percy told me the inspiration for this way of dividing the book, opening with the third person while recounting her subject's past and then switching to the first when describing the present, came from Tracy Kidder's *Strength in What Remains*, an account of a traumatized young doctor from Burundi who makes his way to the United States.) Daniels recedes from view after suggesting to Percy that she, too, is haunted by a demon and needs to have it exorcised. Percy told me that she followed up on this idea "as a means of getting closer to his experience (another move at empathy). I needed to go through the process (or thought I did) for Caleb to accept me as the author of his trauma." At the cultlike ministry of his father-in-law, a Pentecostal in rural Georgia, she submits to a series of rituals, getting in so deep that she feels, and the reader feels, a kind of vertigo, something from a bad dream that suggests the narrator has lost balance and perspective, if temporarily.

For Percy, as with others steeped in the lyric essay approach of some MFA programs, subjective truth trumps traditional journalistic imperatives. The reader doesn't doubt that the events described actually happened, but fact-checking, in this school of writing, is of secondary importance. Empathy and singularity of expression matter more. "They crawled into an area of fern and cedar and dead upright trees." "Caleb picked a gnat out of his eye, wet and dead." His experience of war was "green-lit and strange." Percy's diction, lyric and impressionistic, comes from poetry, not news. *Demon Camp* transcends a common solipsism of these programs, however, by Percy's deep immersion in one man's (very topical) experience. Hers is a jagged, in-your-face depiction of one veteran's nightmare, and the religious and cultural soil that gives it shape. If you don't believe in demons or appreciate her aesthetic, *Demon Camp* may test your patience. Even so, it is exciting to see immersion writing extend in this unnerving new direction.

FINAL THOUGHTS ABOUT FIRST PERSON

All of the works I describe above were reported: the writer went out and learned something, with the idea of writing about it. This reporting, handwritten in notebooks, typed into laptop computers, or captured in cameras, voice recorders, and smartphone apps, typically constitutes the raw material of a book or article. But it may not be the *only* material.

In 2015 Sebastian Junger published an article about PTSD in *Vanity Fair*. Most of it was based upon interviews with anthropologists, counselors, and veterans as well as medical studies and government reports. But it opened with the following two paragraphs (which happen to be the part I remember best about it, a month after my first reading):

> The first time I experienced what I now understand to be post-traumatic stress disorder, I was in a subway station in New York City, where I live. It was almost a year before the attacks of 9/11, and I'd just come back from two months in Afghanistan with Ahmad Shah Massoud, the leader of the Northern Alliance. I was on assignment to write a profile of Massoud, who fought a desperate resistance against the Taliban until they assassinated him two days before 9/11. At one point during my trip we were on a frontline position that his forces had just taken over from the Taliban, and the inevitable counterattack started with an hour-long rocket barrage. All we could do was curl up in the trenches and hope. I felt deranged for days afterward, as if I'd lived through the end of the world.
>
> By the time I got home, though, I wasn't thinking about that or any of the other horrific things we'd seen; I mentally buried all of it until one day, a few months later, when I went into the subway at rush hour to catch the C train downtown. Suddenly I found myself backed up against a metal support column, absolutely convinced I was going to die. There were too many people on the platform, the trains were coming into the station too fast, the lights were too bright, the world was too loud. I couldn't quite explain what was wrong, but I was far more scared than I'd ever been in Afghanistan.

By contrast, Jennifer Percy, though she has reported from Afghanistan, has less experience as a war reporter and does not mention it in her book.

When I was growing up, the first person was largely verboten in journalism, restricted to newspaper columns. Use of the word

"I" was considered a distraction ("we read this for news and information, not to learn about the personal life of the reporter"). News sources, especially in North America, aimed for objectivity, and the first person was an invitation to be subjective. But in the '60s that started to change. Journalism grew more narrative, more literary, and it became clear that a skillful first person voice added new dimensions, new possibilities to writing. Hunter S. Thompson and Tom Wolfe put their first person on the scene in the West Coast happenings of the hippie years. Joan Didion rendered her experiences as a young journalist in New York elegantly in the personal essays of *Slouching towards Bethlehem*. Little by little, the "I" became acceptable in serious nonfiction.

Fast forward—very fast—to today, when writers become accustomed from an early age to first-person public expression on social media and even in academic essays. My position, as a teacher of writing and as an active writer, is that you have to *earn* your first person. Your "I" needs to bring some value to the piece or else it is a distraction. If your topic is addiction and recovery and you have personal experience with those, then *perhaps* your experience deserves a place in the writing: it is, after all, part of the store of what you know about the topic. Your material for a piece of writing may well include things you've read or situations you've witnessed before your reporting or even, as with Junger and Percy, during your reporting. Whether to include this material will depend on the nature of the personal experience, and on the focus of the work.

My favorite sort of reporting for my own writing is experiential, which probably accounts for the way I write my books. Time and again, I've imagined a situation I could put myself into for the purpose of learning about it firsthand and then writing about it. I try to picture a situation somewhat out of the familiar world, and yet topical. Mexican workers, for example: it struck me they were all over the news. And yet little was known, when I wrote *Coyotes*, about the particulars of their lives, much of which, between border crossings, leaving home, and living in a clandestine fashion in the United States, I might learn about by seeing it firsthand. My reporting and my experience, in other words, are often the same thing.

Other immersion writers limit their first person to an introduction or an afterword or, as I've mentioned, leave themselves out of it entirely. John McPhee, like many writers associated with the *New Yorker*, uses the first person to acknowledge his presence in a scene or to otherwise move things along narratively, but seldom to express an opinion or reveal information about himself. Katherine Boo has said,

> As a reader, I sometimes find that the "I" character becomes the character—that the writer can't quite resist trying to make the reader like him just a little better than anyone else in the book. And I think that impedes the reader's ability to connect with people who might be more interesting than the writer, and whose stories are less familiar.

I respect this stance, and have seen that sometimes she's right. (One cure, in my mind, is to fashion a narrator who is not completely likable, who makes instructive mistakes.) But I also think it's often frustrating to read a book-length account of a foreign world, researched by an outsider who immersed herself in it, and learn little or nothing about the challenges of that immersion. One reason is that every on-site researcher changes the story in some way. My confidence in a book or article researched this way is often enhanced by transparency about the reporting; I feel better, in other words, if I can picture Tracy Kidder sitting in that fifth-grade classroom. *Transparency, it is said, is the new objectivity.* Rather than pretend we don't have a bias, don't have an effect on how the story is told, let's be open and self-aware about our leanings and our process. A well-wrought first-person, in my estimation, can be a step toward transparency.

Finally, and particularly in the case of first-person narration, comes a caution over claims. Can we learn about the work of a bricklayer by working alongside him for a week? Certainly—we will understand more than if we never had done it. But can we then say we understand the life of a bricklayer? No, we cannot. The deeper knowing cannot be gleaned from a brief visit.

One Sunday after I had been on the rails for a couple of months, I was feeling lonely and called my aunt in New Jersey, from whose house I had hit the road (just like Kerouac, I'd been thinking). She congratulated me on having figured out how to ride a freight train and declared, "You're a hobo!" I thanked her, said I didn't really think so, and then, after we hung up, thought about how wrong she was. I wasn't a hobo. I wanted to understand hoboes, wanted to learn from hoboes—but already I could appreciate how much I did not want to be one. A hobo knew about loss and disconnection in a deep way that changed a person. A hobo stood for freedom in some people's eyes, but to travel with them was to see their wounds. A hobo couldn't call his family when he was feeling blue, couldn't ask for money for a bus ticket when he wanted to go home.

VI. AFTERMATH

A good recipe for a long life . . . would be to travel
from country to country, culture to culture, language to
language as ever the new resident, the ear ever affronted by
fresh sounds, the senses ever sharp and attention honed. . . .
It is hard to go to sleep on a world you are
struggling to pronounce.

BRUCE BERGER, *The End of the Sherry*

The harder feat for any fieldworker is not getting in; it's leaving.

MATTHEW DESMOND, *Evicted*

One way to think of a book or article is as a custom-made isotope or organism that is being released into the environment for the first time. We have some guesses about what might happen once it's out there, but in truth we don't know. With luck the work will be noticed, will win readers, will make some kind of difference in the world.

Among the people it will almost surely matter to are its subjects—people who, in most cases, will not know exactly what has been written about them until they see it on the page (and may not have known they've been written about at all). For many writers, this is an important moment of reckoning. In most cases, we want our subjects to like our stories—or at the very least to acknowledge that they are true. On the other hand, writing that simply flatters is fluff. Have we properly imagined the desired middle ground?

The task is perhaps easiest in cases where the writer's interests align with those of her sources. A good example of this is

The Immortal Life of Henrietta Lacks, by Rebecca Skloot. The author set out to disinter lost details of the life of Lacks, whose doctors took a biopsy of her cervical cancer cells while she was receiving (free) treatment at Johns Hopkins. The cancer eventually killed Lacks, but her cells lived on: researchers discovered they were a particularly virulent and fast-growing strain . . . ideal, they soon appreciated, for cultivating in the laboratory for research purposes. "HeLa" cells, as they have long been known in the research community, continue to help medical science, a good thing. But what about Lacks' DNA being commercially available to anyone, without her permission, and with no financial benefit to her or her descendants? Lacks' relatives were an important source for Skloot, and some proceeds of her book now go to them; parts of the medical establishment, to their credit, were another important source, and Skloot's work has resulted in lasting reforms that benefit not just Lacks' descendants, but anyone whose DNA might be useful to researchers. In a way, the publication of this kind of book, in which all parties appear to gain, is truly a best-case scenario. For worst case, I might nominate Joe McGinniss' *Fatal Vision,* mentioned earlier in the book.

Projects more typically fall between these two extremes. The subjects of a piece of immersion writing, in most cases, will have a reasonably good idea of what we've written before it is published. The writer may have gone back to them for clarification or verification of certain points; a fact-checker may have, as well. (The better magazines have fact-checkers on staff or working as freelancers. Book publishers typically do not, and many authors of nonfiction books hire their own fact-checkers.)

Preparing our subjects for publication, for example by keeping them in the loop about when we expect the book or article to come out, is generally a good idea, even if we expect they will not be completely pleased when they read it. It is considerate and may imply that we expect them to like it. Even subjects who may be expecting something negative might appreciate the respect. I didn't let New York State's Department of Correctional Services know that I'd written about my employment for *Newjack* until a month or two before publication. They refused, at that point, to even cooperate with fact-checkers from the *New Yorker*. But I also made a personal call to the man who had been superintendent of Sing Sing when I worked there. (He had moved on to a different prison by then.) I told him about the book and my research, and about Albany being unhappy. "Well, did you get everything right?" he asked me. "As far as I know I did," I replied. "Then good luck with it," he said.

But how to prep subjects for publication is not always black and white. A student of mine—a young journalist of promise—was assigned by a major newspaper to write a feature about a local manufacturer of pool tables. For whatever reason, perhaps friendliness, she decided to show a draft to her subjects, and mentioned to her editor that she had. The editor was upset. "They almost killed it!" she told me. Not showing articles to subjects is considered a best practice by many publications, among them our finest newspapers: it protects the paper, and the journalist, from pressure to change something that is truthful, but perhaps not flattering to the subjects.[*]

Immersion projects tend to involve a more complicated calculus when it comes to the days before publication. I have never

---

[*] Fact-checkers sometimes handle this problem by paraphrasing a subject's quote back to them, to check it for accuracy. In other words, instead of saying to a subject, "According to our writer, you said, and I quote, 'After shaking hands with the mayor, I count my fingers to make sure I still have five,'" which gives them the opportunity to tweak the quote or recant, the fact-checker might say, "According to our writer, you said the mayor can't always be trusted."

shown a piece of writing to a subject in advance, but I know of writers I respect who have, mainly with parts of books. (Newspaper and magazine writers should never do this without asking their editor first.) This is typically because a long period of research was involved and the subject played a major part in that research, acting in some ways like a collaborator: giving them a peek will help with accuracy, and may help put them at ease in a way that feels appropriate to the partnership. Short of this, the writer may wish to simply describe the work verbally to her subject. Sometimes it's little things that will upset our subjects, not big ones, and if you can maintain a good relationship with your subject by simply, say, leaving out that story about the time she spilled ketchup on her friend, it might be worth it. A writer who might hope to expand an article into a book feels particular pressure in a situation like this: if the subject is disillusioned by the article, there won't be any book. On the other hand, a writer caters to his subject by omitting substantive and/or critical stories at his peril: our first loyalty must be to the truth and to the reader.

I learned about the "little things" when I wrote a piece for *Travel + Leisure*. The subject was known by some as "cowboy Christmas": the one occasion every summer when rodeo cowboys in northern Wyoming and Montana can take part in three rodeos in a single day (if they drive fast). To fill in my research, I spent a few days beforehand with a bareback rider named Jay. He and his friends were colorful and I enjoyed our travels a lot. I mailed Jay a copy of the magazine after the article came out and followed up with a phone call to hear how he liked it.

His fiancée was noticeably cool on the phone. Jay wasn't in, she said. Well, how did you guys like the piece? I asked. There was a pause. "You didn't have to say he was a cripple!" she declared.

"What?" I said. "I didn't say he was 'a cripple.'"

"Well, you said he walks with a limp," she said. "That sounds like a cripple to me."

"But he does have a limp!" I protested.

"You didn't have to say it," she said bitterly.

In a similar vein, a student of mine profiled a delivery man he had gotten to know at a hamburger joint where both of them worked. The delivery man had been a professor in Mexico and, among other things, showed his erudition by his appreciation of the architecture of buildings he'd deliver to; he was always snapping photos of them. He was reluctant to smile, said my student, having lost teeth after biting into something hard at the restaurant. The restaurant's manager, quoted in the story, mentioned that the company's health insurance hadn't covered the dental expense.

My student placed the piece on the website of a national magazine where, unfortunately, the folks in "corporate" saw it. They took the manager to task. The manager told my student that the delivery man's job, and maybe the manager's own, were at risk if the story wasn't changed. Distraught, my student asked his editor if the change could be made: he had never wanted to make anyone lose his job. The editor kindly said yes; crisis averted.

Is it always that easy for a writer who has second thoughts, or discovers a mistake, to fix things? In a printed magazine or newspaper, the answer is no, except for a printed correction that runs later. In a printed book, the answer is no—unless a writer is lucky enough that the book will have a second printing, in which case publishers will sometimes agree to making slight changes. At online publications, of course, it's doable though by no means automatic: editors will be loath to walk back a material fact touching on a matter of public interest, just because a source objects. (If the publication does agree to a change, sometimes an editor's note will be appended that explains it, so that attentive readers won't feel some kind of cover-up has taken place.)

vvv

Apart from the question of how a given person will respond to your writing, there is the question of whether readers generally will respond—of critical and popular reception. Anne Fadiman's book, *The Spirit Catches You and You Fall Down*, cites a quote variously attributed to the Talmud, Immanuel Kant, and Shirley MacLaine: "We do not see the world as it is. We see it as we are." Thus, Fadiman told my class, "Hmong readers think this is a book about the Hmong. Doctors who read this book think it's about the difficulties of cross-cultural medicine. People who do refugee resettlement think it's a book about the challenges of refugee resettlement."

A somewhat grittier example is a story I wrote about a Minnesota murderer, Roy Wahlberg, and his victim's family, named Goedderz. The family had filed a civil suit against Wahlberg after he had done his time, having heard he made money on a software product while in prison. Wahlberg reached a settlement with them. But he told me, as we hung out various times after his release, that their hatred weighed on him. For their part, the family was happy to tell me their story—but also suspicious that I'd been spending time with Wahlberg. I know they were wondering whose side I was on, and wouldn't really know until the article came out. I tried hard to be evenhanded when I wrote it but, as I sent the link and mailed printed copies of the magazine to both sides, I was pretty sure neither would be delighted.

Wahlberg, back in prison when he received it, was unhappy about certain details but conceded there was nothing in the piece that could be called "incorrect." Then the phone rang—the victim's older brother, a man who had taken me fishing in Ely, Minnesota, and had described the many bar brawls he'd been in. He was livid; I could picture his hands forming fists. I listened while he vented and then said something to the effect of, "Well, that's strange. Because I was just speaking to Wahlberg, and he's also quite unhappy."

"He is?" I enumerated Wahlberg's complaints, and the caller digested them. "Well, I guess it's not all that bad then," he finally said.

vvv

Things we publish make an almost instantaneous move from an existence inside our heads, surrounded by our attention only, to an independent existence quite outside of us. As more than one writer has noticed, once published, our writing "belongs to the world." We can wish it good luck—and might be called on to defend it—but essentially on publication it begins a life of its own. We wrote it, but it's no longer ours. Hopefully it will have a long life—or at least not a short one—and make a good kind of difference.

To me, immersion writing is a special category because of its implicit message: it says *we can come to understand each other*. As Alex Kotlowitz wrote me, "I've always felt that empathy is the centripetal force both of storytelling and of community—and so the power of nonfiction immersive storytelling can in the end serve to connect us, to build community." In the best cases, this goal of understanding the other will work against tribal ignorance and animosity. It can stand as an example of the possibility of diverse groups speaking to each other, of dialogue and hope. The research can be difficult and take a long time, but I think that writers attach a singular kind of pride to their authorship of immersion writing. It's the opposite of name-calling.

As for what comes next: Finishing a book can be a major life event for a writer. Even long articles can represent a year of work, and completion for many people is bittersweet. There's a sense of achievement, yes, but also an empty place inside where the project once resided. Some people are immediately on to the next. Others wait for the vacuum to attract new ideas. Still other writers are spent; that last project was enough!

For me, deeply immersive experiences have been both fascinating and disorienting. Spending long periods of time with people different from ourselves can affect our own sense of identity. When I return to my regular life, I think of it not like shedding a skin but like releasing the tension in a rubber band. My immersion stretched my somewhat flexible sense of self; returning home, the rubber band snaps back into its previous shape mostly . . . but not entirely. After all, rubber bands once stretched aren't exactly the way they were to begin with. They hold more. And so I usually feel: larger, in a good way, from having been stretched.

The writing lets me think about it, process it. My authorial voice needs to stand back from the experience and comment on it, and it's that new shape that informs the book. Finishing a piece of immersion writing signals in a way the end of that process of reconstituting myself, rebuilding, absorbing, and processing. It readies me for the next.

ACKNOWLEDGMENTS

I thank Jay Leibold, Edward J. Davis, Anne Hermann, Robert Boynton, Mary Laur, Nicholas Dawidoff, Brooke Kroeger, J. C. Hallman, Jenny Gavacs, Eli Epstein, Kelsey Kudak, Danielle Mackey, Rick Larson, Charles Seife, Dale Maharidge, Arlene Stein, Robert Moor, Jessica Benko, Mathew Rodriguez, and my students at New York University and the Bread Loaf Writers' Conference. And thanks especially to my wife and forever editor, Margot Guralnick.

ANNOTATED BIBLIOGRAPHY

Included in this bibliography are works that I consider significant examples of immersion writing, many of them mentioned in the text. Within each section, they are organized chronologically by date of publication (earliest first, most recent last).

BOOKS OF IMMERSION WRITING

Sir Richard Francis Burton, *Personal Narrative of a Pilgrimage to Al-Madinah and Meccah in Two Volumes* (1855–56). A foundational example of immersion writing, in which an Oxford dropout with a facility for language and love of the foreign disguises himself as a Muslim (even getting circumcised), and joins would-be hajjis on a trip to Mecca.

Nellie Bly, *Ten Days in a Mad-House* (1887). Bly, a newspaper "stunt girl" who attracted readers by placing herself in interesting or difficult situations, succeeded in getting herself committed to a New York City insane asylum for ten days. Her account of the poor and ineffective treatment she received riveted the nation and prompted reforms.

George Orwell, *Down and Out in Paris and London* (1933). For his first book, the great writer spent weeks among the destitute of two great cities. More celebrated for the concept than for the execution, it nevertheless shows the power of experience to change a narrator's point of view.

James Agee and Walker Evans, *Let Us Now Praise Famous Men* (1941). To cast light on the conditions of Southern sharecroppers living in poverty, dramatist Agee, accompanied by photographer Evans, lived with three different families over the course of eight weeks. Deeply felt, oddly organized, and passionately written, the book reads like part documentary and part experimental fever dream.

John Hersey, *Hiroshima* (1946). Hershey's classic book begins on the morning the atomic bomb was dropped, immediately killing over 100,000 people, and follows the lives of six who survived.

John Howard Griffin, *Black Like Me* (1961). In this bestselling work of immersion journalism ever, Griffin darkened his hair and skin and left his home in rural Texas—where segregationists had fought to keep black children out of white schools—to travel the rural South for a black magazine (which had a white publisher).

Gay Talese, *The Bridge: The Building of the Verrazano-Narrows Bridge* (1964). This multifaceted portrait examines the work of engineers and the displacement of neighborhoods—but it is remembered particularly for its focus on ironworkers "whose fingerprints are on the bolts and beams" of the soaring edifice.

Truman Capote, *In Cold Blood* (1966). A milestone in the use of narrative techniques in nonfiction storytelling, Capote's book recounts the murder of four members of a Kansas farm family, the Clutters, by two men they didn't know. Its empathy for the murderers, Dick Hickok and, particularly, Perry Smith, also broke new ground; he portrayed their lives from before the crimes to during and after, including their execution by hanging.

George Plimpton, *Paper Lion: Confessions of a Last-String Quarterback* (1966). This best-known of Plimpton's participatory forays into the world of professional sports shows the literary man-about-town taking part in preseason training with the Detroit Lions football team. His other books include *Out of My League* (1961, about baseball), *The Bogey Man* (1967, golf), and *Open Net* (1985, hockey)—but *Paper Lion*, which uses the author's own incompetence to comic effect, stands out as practically synonymous with "immersion writing" to many readers of a certain age.

Hunter S. Thompson, *Hell's Angels: The Strange and Terrible Saga of the Outlaw Motorcycle Gangs* (1967). In the 1960s, the Hell's Angels were a powerful and scary gang. Thompson, writing for *Rolling Stone* from San Francisco, leveraged some acquaintances and was able to spend time with them—not riding, but at meet-ups both giant and small. This was a feat in itself, but Thompson's achievement goes further with his singular writing style, which captures the feel of the group and the fear of outsiders.

Tom Wolfe, *The Electric Kool-Aid Acid Test* (1968). Wolfe joined novelist/guru Ken Kesey and his followers, the Merry Pranksters, in an LSD-fueled bus ride across the United States and in other "consciousness-raising" adventures. The subject matter often feels of a piece with Wolfe's New Journalism stylistic experiments: vivid, long sentences, some italics on every page, and narration that channels the mindset of his subjects.

John McPhee, *The Crofter and the Laird* (1970). The dean of *New Yorker* nonfiction writers, McPhee took his family to his ancestral Scottish island. They rented a cottage, the children entered a local school, and McPhee prepared this portrait of a traditional place meeting the modern era.

Timothy Crouse, *The Boys on the Bus* (1973). Crouse, then a reporter for *Rolling Stone*, joined the journalists covering the 1972 American presidential campaign—and then wrote not about the candidates but about his colorful colleagues. A classic of political reporting that heightened awareness of "pack journalism."

Tom Wolfe, *The Right Stuff* (1979). Wolfe's book, a huge bestseller and the basis for a movie, both lionizes and demystifies the military test pilots who became America's first astronauts, as well as those (like Chuck Yeager) who were not chosen. The title refers to the "brotherhood's" ethic of bravery and boldness.

Cameron Crowe, *Fast Times at Ridgemont High* (1981). In his first book, 22-year-old writer-turned-filmmaker Crowe returned to high school in southern California on undercover assignment for *Rolling Stone*. He recounted the year from the perspective of six students in hilarious, novelistic fashion. Sympathetic and original, the book captures the passion and daftness of high school—as did the more famous movie of the same name, which Crowe wrote and directed.

David Owen, *High School: Undercover with the Class of '80* (1981). The *New Yorker* writer, then 24, enrolled as a senior at a Connecticut high school for most of a semester. Uncomfortable with the deception, he kept himself emotionally at arm's length but drew amusing critiques of certain teachers and aspects of public school education.

Stanley Booth, *Dance with the Devil: The Rolling Stones and Their Times* (1984). Known for writing about the blues, journalist Booth signed on with the Stones in 1969 to follow them on tour. He got in so deep that the book took years to write; but the result is incandescent and inspiring.

Lis Harris, *Holy Days: The World of the Hasidic Family* (1985). Harris, a *New Yorker* writer who suspects her family of denying the Hasidim in her family tree, goes looking for traditional Jewish life among the Lubavitchers of Crown Heights, Brooklyn.

Gunter Wallraff, *Lowest of the Low* (1988). Europe's most celebrated undercover journalist passes as a Turkish guest worker in a German steel factory and in a McDonald's restaurant, and as a human guinea pig in drug trials in this, his most famous book. *The Undesirable Journalist* (1978), easier to find, contains shorter investigative pieces that make rightists, German police, and a Portuguese archbishop look bad.

Yoram Binur, *My Enemy, My Self* (1989). A journalist accustomed to covering Palestine as an Israeli takes advantage of his Sephardic background and fluent Arabic to pass as a Palestinian—in Israel, the West Bank, and Gaza. Binur is open and unflinching in his examination of his country, and his own weaknesses.

Tracy Kidder, *Among Schoolchildren* (1989). The title says it well: Kidder spent a school year in the fifth-grade classroom of a seasoned teacher in Holyoke, Massachusetts, vividly capturing the humanity of all.

H. G. Bissinger, *Friday Night Lights: A Town, A Team, and a Dream* (1990). Bissinger moved his family to Odessa, Texas, for a school year to document the local civil religion. The result was a big bestseller and an even better-known television series by the same name.

Alex Kotlowitz, *There Are No Children Here: The Story of Two Boys Growing Up in the Other America* (1991). For more than two years, Kotlowitz chronicled the lives of

Lafeyette and Pharoah Rivers in and around Chicago's Henry Horner Homes, a place of pervasive violence.

Bill Buford, *Among the Thugs* (1993). Instead of simply condemning Britain's nefarious football hooligans, Buford hung out with them, traveling to pubs and overseas matches in a search for meaning behind mayhem.

Bob Reiss, *Frequent Flyer: One Plane, One Passenger, and the Spectacular Feat of Commercial Flight* (1994). Reiss's 72 hours in one of Delta's Airlines jets, as it hopscotches 15,000 miles across the United States and stops in Japan, is shorter than most immersions—but the larger story here, researched over a much longer period, is how an airline works.

Michael Winerip, *9 Highland Road: Sane Living for the Mentally Ill* (1994). The story of residents of a supervised group home on Long Island is told with insight and respect.

Madeleine Blais, *In These Girls, Hope Is a Muscle* (1995). A season in the life of a girl's high school basketball team, "nice girls from a nice town," culminating in a chance to prove themselves at the state championships.

Jon Krakauer, *Into Thin Air: A Personal Account of the Mount Everest Disaster* (1997). Intending to write a magazine article about commercial expeditions up Everest, Krakauer finds himself in the middle of a mountaineering debacle and human tragedy.

Anne Fadiman, *The Spirit Catches You and You Fall Down: A Hmong Child, Her American Doctors, and the Collision of Two Cultures* (1998). Fadiman turns the story of Lia Lee, a child of Hmong immigrants in Merced, California, with a grave seizure disorder, into a parable of miscommunication between modern medicine and traditional beliefs.

Tony Horwitz, *Confederates in the Attic: Dispatches from the Unfinished Civil War* (1998). One of the several ways in which journalist Horwitz explores Southern feeling about the Civil War is to join a team of "super hardcore" Civil War reenactors. He drills with the squad one weekend in Virginia, later joining them and 8,000 others in a mock Battle of the Wilderness.

John McPhee, *Annals of the Former World* (1998). This compilation of McPhee's five books about North American geology, researched via road trips with noted geologists, amounts to an immersion in the geologists' world.

Barbara Ehrenreich, *Nickel and Dimed: On (Not) Getting By in America* (2001). In this well-titled bestseller, Ehrenreich aimed to show firsthand the difficulty of surviving in America as an unskilled worker by trying it herself. She spent one month each as a waitress in Key West, a housekeeper in Portland, Maine, and a floor worker at a Wal-Mart in Minneapolis.

Rubén Martínez, *Crossing Over: A Mexican Family on the Migrant Trail* (2002). Following the members of a single extended family on their journeys from rural Mexico into the United States, Martínez tells a new kind of immigration story, at once hopeful and dystopic.

Adrian Nicole LeBlanc, *Random Family: Love, Drugs, Trouble, and Coming of Age in the Bronx* (2003). Covering the trial of a drug kingpin in New York, LeBlanc found herself intrigued by the lives of the women in his life and, after his conviction, followed them as they carried on with their lives in the South Bronx and then upstate—for more than ten years.

Norah Vincent, *Self-Made Man: One Woman's Year Disguised as a Man* (2006). A smart and worthwhile book even if you think you know a lot about being a man. What the subtitle doesn't reveal is what an adept researcher and large-hearted writer Vincent is, nor how the experience messed her up. (See her book, *Voluntary Madness*, below.)

Lauren Kessler, *Dancing with Rose: Finding Life in the Land of Alzheimer's* (2007). Author Kessler found employment as a caregiver to people with Alzheimer's, to better appreciate the disease and its place in our lives.

Joe Mackall, *Plain Secrets: An Outsider among the Amish* (2007). This immersion began organically, as Mackall grew curious about his new neighbors in rural Ohio. Eventually his life came to intersect with theirs in many ways; a humanizing primer on the Amish.

Dudley Clendinen, *A Place Called Canterbury: Tales of the New Old Age in America* (2008). Part immersion journalism, part memoir of a man's relationship with his mother, Clendinen's book recounts his many visits to her assisted living tower in Tampa Bay during the (busy) last years of her life.

Jeff Sharlet, *The Family: The Secret Fundamentalism at the Heart of American Power* (2008). Sharlet reports on fundamentalist Christians in government, and their animating ideology, after living at their estate just outside Washington, DC.

Bill Wasik, ed., *Submersion Journalism: Reporting in the Radical First Person from Harper's Magazine* (2008). Harper's has a long tradition of immersion reporting; collected here are 13 long articles, including Ken Silverstein's withering undercover setup of lobbyists, "Their Men in Washington."

Rich Benjamin, *Searching for Whitopia: An Improbable Journey to the Heart of White America* (2009). Benjamin, an African American and researcher at the think tank Demos, says that white people are seeking refuge from ever-more-multicultural America in small towns and exurbs that are predominantly, even extremely, white. Over two years, he lives in three of them.

Tracy Kidder, *Strength in What Remains* (2009). This account of a traumatized young doctor from Burundi who makes his way to the United States, where he knows nobody and where his training counts for nothing, starts as a horror story and becomes, in Kidder's hands, a tale of lasting beauty.

Nick Reding, *Methland: The Death and Life of an American Small Town* (2009). Journalist Reding recounts the ravages of methamphetamine on a depressed town in Iowa, both on those who take the drug and on those who live around them.

Kevin Roose, *The Unlikely Disciple: A Sinner's Semester at America's Holiest University* (2009). A sophomore at Brown University, Roose enrolled at the Rev. Jerry

Falwell's Liberty University—a change that practically qualifies as a semester abroad. He appreciates the humanity in his new classmates, but the lasting impression is of the gulfs that divide them. Thoughtful and entertaining.

Norah Vincent, *Voluntary Madness: My Year Lost and Found in the Loony Bin* (2009). The immersion research for Vincent's previous book (see *Self-Made Man*, above) wreaked havoc on her psyche, one reason she checked herself into not just one "bin," but several: a public hospital in New York City, a Catholic clinic in the Midwest, and a private outpatient program in the South.

Gabriel Thompson, *Working in the Shadows: A Year of Doing the Jobs (Most) Americans Won't Do* (2010). Focusing on the kinds of jobs held by the undocumented, Thompson spent a year working in Arizona lettuce fields, at an Alabama chicken factory, in a New York City restaurant kitchen, and in a florist's shop.

Sebastian Junger, *War* (2010). Junger's account of several visits to a particularly dangerous American outpost in Afghanistan's Korengal Valley, and his account of the lives of soldiers in a platoon deployed there over 15 months, makes for gripping, empathetic reading. By the author of *The Perfect Storm*.

Theo Padnos, *Undercover Muslim: A Journey into Yemen* (2011). Padnos enrolled in religious schools in Yemen in order to understand the wave of young Muslims from the West doing the same. The book illuminates much about them and the country, while leaving the character of the author a bit of a puzzle. (Padnos, now named Peter Theo Curtis, gained notoriety after his release in 2014 from two years of captivity by the Nusra Front, in Syria.)

Tracie McMillan, *The American Way of Eating: Undercover at Walmart, Applebee's, Farm Fields and the Dinner Table* (2012). Journalist McMillan worked three jobs connected to food, living exclusively off her wages, in order to examine the larger system of food production and marketing in the United States.

Katherine Boo, *Behind the Beautiful Forevers: Life, Death, and Hope in a Mumbai Undercity* (2012). Boo's account of life in a Mumbai slum, and the saga of a family accused of murder in the death-by-burning of their disabled next-door neighbor, has won almost universal acclaim.

Nicholas Dawidoff, *Collision Low Crossers: A Year Inside the Turbulent World of NFL Football* (2013). Building on a cover profile of coach Rex Ryan in the *New York Times Magazine*, Dawidoff received permission to follow the team for an entire season—his access included even a parking place and locker at their "facility" in Florham Park, New Jersey. Sophisticated insight into the ideas, personalities, and processes behind major league football.

Alice Goffman, *On the Run: Fugitive Life in an American City* (2014). This ethnography, based on years of participant observation by sociologist Goffman in a poor neighborhood in Philadelphia, shows how the legal system keeps many young black men in a fairly constant state of flight. Particularly compelling is the 50-page "Appendix: A Methodological Note," a condensed narrative account of her research.

Suki Kim, *Without You, There Is No Us: My Time with the Sons of North Korea's Elite* (2014). Marketed as a memoir, this illuminating account of teaching English for six months in Pyongyang overlaps with first-person investigative journalism.

Jennifer Percy, *Demon Camp: A Soldier's Exorcism* (2014). Percy, wanting to understand PTSD, went deep inside the mind of an American soldier tortured by his experience in Afghanistan. Then she spent time with a Pentecostal group that believes the demons associated with such trauma can literally be exorcised. Views of a nightmare, lyrically rendered.

Matthew Desmond, *Evicted: Poverty and Profit in the American City* (2016). Sociologist Desmond, winner of a MacArthur "genius" grant, based himself in a trailer park and a rooming house in Milwaukee, and learned about eviction from both landlords and tenants. Rigorously researched and deftly written, with a moving personal reflection on field work at the end ("About This Project").

PEACE CORPS MEMOIRS

George Packer, *The Village of Waiting* (1984). On not making a big difference in Togo.

Peter Hessler, *River Town: Two Years on the Yangtze* (2001). A Princeton grad who speaks Chinese is assigned to instruct middle-aged English teachers in a poor industrial city; he declares, "It was hard for me to imagine a better job."

Tom Bissell, *Chasing the Sea: Lost among the Ghosts of Empire in Central Asia* (2003). Bissell, who left the Peace Corps before finishing his gig, revisits Uzbekistan—and a sense of his own failure—while on a magazine assignment.

Sarah Erdman, *Nine Hills to Nambonkaha: Two Years in the Heart of an African Village* (2003). A soulful, literary passage through village life in the Ivory Coast.

Kris Holloway, *Monique and the Mango Rains: Two Years with a Midwife in Mali* (2006). A tight focus on her host, a midwife whose job involves her in life and death on a daily basis, keeps this account centered on the social forces that appear to converge to keep women pregnant, poor, and unhealthy.

ARTICLE-LENGTH IMMERSION WRITING

Susan Orlean, "All Mixed Up" (*New Yorker*, June 22, 1992). A closely-observed look at a bustling independent grocery store in Jackson Heights, Queens, that offers thousands of items at a tiny markup to people from all over the world. Collected in Orlean's *My Kind of Place: Travel Stories from a Woman Who's Been Everywhere* (2004).

Lawrence Otis Graham, "Invisible Man" (*New York* magazine, August 17, 1992). A Harvard-educated lawyer who is African American goes to work as a $7-an-hour busboy at the Greenwich Country Club. Collected in Graham's volume of essays, *Member of the Club* (1995).

Susan Orlean, "The American Man, Age Ten" (*Esquire*, December 1992).

A brilliant, idiosyncratic portrait of an American 10-year-old. Collected in *The Bullfighter Checks Her Makeup* (2001).

Matthew Power, "Mississippi Drift: River Vagrants in the Age of Wal-Mart" (*Harper's*, March 2008). Floating the great waterway on a makeshift raft with a crew of punk anarchists.

Amy Harmon, "Navigating Love and Autism" (*New York Times*, December 26, 2011). An intimate, step-by-step account of two college-age people with autism getting together and staying together.

Luke Mogelson, "The Dream Boat" (*New York Times Magazine*, November 17, 2013). Writer Mogelson, and photographer Joel Van Houdt, traveled to Indonesia and there posed as refugees from the Republic of Georgia in order to accompany a boatload of Iranians hoping to gain entry to Australia via Christmas Island.

MY OWN BOOKS

Rolling Nowhere: Riding the Rails with America's Hoboes (1984). Still a college student, I take to the rails to learn about those who live on and around freight trains.

Coyotes: A Journey Across Borders with America's Mexican Migrants (1987). The people I met on the rails who best fit the classic definition of "hobo" were Mexican. Starting in Arizona, and with a long stay in Mexico, I travel around the United States with migrants my own age.

Whiteout: Lost in Aspen (1991). Does immersion writing work among the wealthy? I wear many hats in Aspen in an attempt to find out.

Newjack: Guarding Sing Sing (2000). Looking for an up-close view of the prison crisis, I become a correction officer.

The Routes of Man: Travels in the Paved World (2010). A passage along six roads that profoundly change the places they're in, researched by spending time with drivers and others in China, Peru, Kashmir, Kenya, Lagos, and the West Bank.

MY RELEVANT ARTICLES

"The Road Is Very Unfair: Trucking Across Africa in the Age of AIDS" (*New Yorker*, August 16, 1993). Early in the epidemic, truck drivers were identified as likely spreaders of the disease. I took a long trip with a convoy of Kenyan drivers, from Mombasa to Burundi, to learn more.

"The Hand-Off" (*New York Times Magazine*, May 8, 1994). Before the advent of anti-retroviral drugs, it looked like the AIDS epidemic would create a whole generation of American orphans. I tell the story of a sick mom looking for a replacement, basically—someone to care for her daughter once she's gone.

"The Way of All Flesh: Undercover in an Industrial Slaughterhouse" (*Harper's*, May 2013). To understand the world of slaughter, I became a USDA red meat inspector, assigned to a Cargill Meat Solutions factory in rural Nebraska.

BOOKS ABOUT WRITING

James Spradley, *Participant Observation* (1980). This book, published on the eve of my undergraduate journey among tramps, helps explain what ethnographers are looking for, and how they find it. I carried it with me.

Vivian Gornick, *The Situation and the Story: The Art of Personal Narrative* (2002). Essays toward a theory of narration in first-person nonfiction, by an admired memoirist and critic.

Jack Hart, *Storycraft: The Complete Guide to Writing Narrative Nonfiction* (2011). An engaging and literate how-to for writers of narrative nonfiction.

Brooke Kroeger, *Undercover Reporting: The Truth About Deception* (2012). A comprehensive history useful also as an idea book, chock-full of examples of enterprising writers who saw a way to better the world by jumping into the action themselves.

Tracy Kidder and Richard Todd, *Good Prose: The Art of Nonfiction* (2013). Seasoned and sage advice.

INDEX